Early Learning through Play

Early Learning through Play

Library Programming for Diverse Communities

Kristin Grabarek and Mary R. Lanni

LIBRARIES UNLIMITED™
An Imprint of ABC-CLIO, LLC
Santa Barbara, California • Denver, Colorado

Copyright © 2019 by Kristin Grabarek and Mary R. Lanni

Library of Congress Cataloging in Publication Control Number: 2019001507

ISBN: 978-1-4408-6582-4 (paperback)
    978-1-4408-6583-1 (ebook)

23 22 21 20 19   1 2 3 4 5

This book is also available as an eBook.

Libraries Unlimited
An Imprint of ABC-CLIO, LLC

ABC-CLIO, LLC
147 Castilian Drive
Santa Barbara, California 93117
www.abc-clio.com

This book is printed on acid-free paper ∞

Manufactured in the United States of America

The publisher has done its best to make sure the instructions and/or recipes in this book are correct. However, users should apply judgment and experience when preparing recipes, especially parents and teachers working with young people. The publisher accepts no responsibility for the outcome of any recipe included in this volume and assumes no liability for, and is released by readers from, any injury or damage resulting from the strict adherence to, or deviation from, the directions and/or recipes herein. The publisher is not responsible for any reader's specific health or allergy needs that may require medical supervision, nor for any adverse reactions to the recipes contained in this book. All yields are approximations.

To my daughter, Stella Grace, whom I carried while writing this book; and to my son, Wesley David, who inspired so much of my work in the first place.

—Kristin

To my daughter, Ava Róisín, who was born as this book took shape: may play be the great work of your childhood.

—Mary

Contents

ONE

Introduction

WHAT IS EARLY LEARNING?

"Early learning," or "early literacy," as it is sometimes known, has become something of a buzzword in public libraries and across our country in recent years. We are beginning to recognize the fact that many children are entering school unprepared for the social and intellectual requirements that entails, and often those children are not reading on grade level by third grade.

Third grade is a critical marker in students' careers. As it is popular to say, up to third grade, children are learning to read. After third grade, children are reading to learn. Children who find themselves behind with third-grade reading struggle the entire rest of their school careers to catch up to grade-level work in *all subjects*. This struggle then in turn contributes to significant learning attrition in high school.

This lack of high school success can lead to low-paying jobs and low quality of life after students leave school. In order to prevent this, the focus on learning has turned to the earliest years, particularly those leading up to third grade, as the place to begin improving the lives of children. For the purposes of this book, we define early learning as learning that happens between ages zero and five.

This is indeed a critical time period for learning! The Harvard Center for the Developing Child offers this intriguing fact: "90% of a child's brain development happens before age 5." Now, please do not panic. It is never too late to learn. This fact simply emphasizes that the younger a learner is, the easier the learning is. Consider how many times you or a friend has observed a toddler and remarked something like, "Their brains are little sponges!"

This jump start on childhood learning has to do with learning pathways within the brain. Our brains create learning pathways even before we are born. Each time a child has an experience—that is, seeing, tasting, touching, smelling, or hearing—the learning pathways multiply and strengthen. Each different experience creates a new learning pathway, while repeated experiences strengthen existing ones. Learning pathways increase and increase, strengthen and strengthen, throughout babyhood, toddlerhood, and childhood.

Around age five or six, the brains of our young learners begin to innately understand that they do not need each and every learning pathway they have developed. For example, consider how many of us as adults could list out 10 different types of dinosaurs off the top of our heads. Now find a precocious four-year-old and challenge him or her to do the same; you will likely have a list of even more than 10! This knowledge is a pathway in a young learner's brain but is not exactly necessary to retain into adulthood or even adolescence. Our brains, then, do us the natural favor of pruning our learning pathways, again around age five or six.

This natural pruning means two things, one positive and one a bit challenging. On the bright side, our learning pathways become smooth, streamlined, and confident. Without a jumble of knowledge, the knowledge we do have is reinforced through practice, repetition, and frequent use. All of us know how to count, can recite the days of the week in order, and sing the alphabet song out loud; far more of us are able to do this than are able to recite the names of 10 dinosaurs. This is because these sets of knowledge were important learning pathways, and our brain retained them and strengthened them so that we can use them throughout our lives.

The second outcome provides us with a bit of a challenge. Concentrating on retaining and strengthening important learning pathways comes at the expense of easily creating new learning pathways. For example, consider how many of us have mastered our primary language, whatever it may be. Now consider difficulties encountered while trying to learn a second language as an adolescent or an adult. This is a frequently cited example of the increasing difficulty of learning that comes with age. While our brain is preserving our important learning pathways, it is doing so at the expense of creating new ones with ease.

This simply means that learning from ages zero through five is of critical importance. The more learning pathways we can enable our young learners to create, the more knowledge they will have inside their brains when the pruning begins. Furthermore, the more learning pathways that exist when children start kindergarten, the more able they will be to retain critical knowledge by strengthening existing pathways, rather than having to face the challenge of building new pathways after their brains have begun the pruning process.

This is the particular situation we refer to when discussing school readiness. We want our young learners to enter kindergarten with as many learning pathways as possible to ensure that they are ready for the social and intellectual requirements of their school career. The critical time period to build these learning pathways is the ages between birth and preschool.

PUBLIC LIBRARY'S ROLE IN EARLY LEARNING

Librarians have been watching the information on the importance of kindergarten readiness and school success come in without surprise. In fact, librarians in general have long recognized the importance of learning and the ways in which libraries can support learners.

To back up a bit for a wider perspective: public libraries are designed and built to facilitate lifelong learning. This certainly includes early learning, as well as learning throughout a student's school career. Not only do libraries innately provide these opportunities, but librarians also intentionally seek out ways to support learning.

For example, before the early learning trend began to sweep our country, the trend was a focus on summer learning loss. Educators, parents, caregivers, and other stakeholders recognized the fact that, without learning opportunities, students would lose a significant amount of the knowledge they had learned during the previous school year over the course of the summer months. The result of the "summer slide," as some refer to this phenomenon, was that teachers had to spend weeks at the beginning of each school year assisting students in catching up to where they were, academically, at the end of the prior school year. This set the whole learning process behind for the school year, compounding the difficulty in keeping up with learning standards for years to come.

Public libraries recognized this gap in academic enrichment and did what they could to help bridge it. Summer reading and learning programs were developed by public librarians to address this growing concern, many of which date back to the 1950s, and some even to the 1930s! Students could visit their public library to learn by reading and/or participating in learning opportunities and be rewarded with incentives for their effort to retain their school knowledge. This work simultaneously prepared them to enter the next school year ready to learn at grade level. Vibrant summer reading and learning programs still thrive today, and their continued existence demonstrates not only the need for such programming but also the critical role public librarians have played for decades to ensure that students have every possible opportunity to thrive.

Perhaps even more well known than summer reading programs, though, are public libraries' well-loved storytimes. Just the word "storytime" often evokes the image of a bespeckled librarian in a rocking chair, reading aloud to a roomful of toddlers snuggled into the laps of their mommies. This mental image of a library storytime is dated for a reason; storytimes have been a pillar of public library services for generations.

Like summer reading and learning programs, the continued existence of storytimes demonstrates their importance to the communities libraries serve. Often, storytimes are the only year-round early learning enrichment available to the entire community free of charge. Libraries in areas of nearly every income level provide some kind of storytime event during the week, particularly because of the impacts these programs have on children and their families.

These impacts may be simplistic when described, but they provide long-lasting positive results for participating children and families. For one, storytimes offer a bonding experience between children and their caregivers. Parents and other caregivers are children's first teachers. The closer children feel to these caregivers, the more they are likely to learn from them.

Brain chemistry plays a critical role in the way children learn. When cortisol, the stress hormone, is pervasively present due to unstable family life or other situations in which a child's basic needs are not being met, it is much more difficult for the child to learn. Parts of a child's brain remain inactive, and the focus and attention needed to build neural pathways are diverted into ensuring basic survival. However, when oxytocin, the "feel-good" hormone, is present, learning occurs much more readily. A child with his or her basic needs (food, shelter, safety) being met, and one with close relationships with parents and other caregivers, is much more likely to experience floods of dopamine through his or her system. Positive experiences are likely to be repeated, and this repetition is what makes new neural pathways stronger.

Storytimes also foster a love of reading from a very young age. Librarians demonstrate during storytimes that books are fun and that reading books together is a fun thing to do! Learning to read, and being able to read, is of critical importance to school success, as we discussed previously. A child motivated to learn to read is likely the one who loves books, and storytimes certainly facilitate this love of books.

It is clear, then, that the truths about children's love of learning and reading and how that influences their success in school have been apparent to librarians for some time. However, as with many large-scale, systemic challenges, truly changing negative outcomes to positive ones relies on the support and participation of our society, not just one or two professions within our society. Now that our society is aware of the learning needs of our youngest children and how early learning contributes to school success, librarians' work to address such challenges has become more commonplace and better understood, making it easier, then, to articulate and accomplish.

This acknowledgment of librarians' work in the learning process is not to reduce or belittle the role of the family in the early learning process. As a child's first teacher, parents and caregivers primarily shoulder the responsibility of ensuring that their child be both properly prepared for and later succeed in school. What public libraries do, then, is help ease that load by providing meaningful programs and enrichment for children and the adults who care for them.

EVERY CHILD READY TO READ (ECRR1 AND ECRR2) @ YOUR LIBRARY

One of the most notable efforts of librarians to enhance the programming libraries offer to support families was the creation of something called Every Child Ready to Read @ Your Library, or ECRR, which was introduced in its first iteration in 2004 ("Home Page"). Essentially, this campaign quantified the work that librarians had long been doing when offering a traditional storytime. ECRR focused on six main target areas that were determined to be critical to preparing young children to enter school. These six target areas were Phonological Awareness, Narrative Skills,* Print Motivation,* Vocabulary, Letter Knowledge, and Print Awareness (Celano 30–35).

---

* Since the creation of ECRR1, Narrative Skills and Print Motivation have been combined into one skill: Background Knowledge. For the purposes of this explanation, we are utilizing the original terminology.

- **Phonological Awareness:** Ability to hear and play with the smaller sounds in words (ECRR Chart).

  Rhyming books, particularly those by Dr. Seuss, are excellent examples of how this awareness can be fostered. Although many of Dr. Seuss's words are made up (e.g., Sneetch), they are words that are easy to rhyme. This provides opportunity to then practice the sounds that make up those rhymes and are found in other, real, words. Nonsense songs like Raffi's "Apples and Bananas" are another good example of this, as they again repeat the sounds that make up all words by making that practice fun.

- **Narrative Skills*:** This includes conceptual thinking about books and stories, being able to determine the beginning, middle, and end (story structure), and being able to replicate that structure independently (ECRR Chart).

  In storytime sessions at the library or at home, readers can ask for a retelling of the story from the participants through guided questions. For example, "who did we meet at the beginning of the story?" requires participants to place in order the characters they met to determine who was the first. This can happen at home as well, as families recount the activities of their day: "And then what did we do?"

- **Print Motivation*:** Understanding the uses of books and enjoying reading them (ECRR Chart).

  Publishers do an excellent job of garnering children's attention to the covers and pages of their books by using bright, vibrant colors and exciting characters like dinosaurs, princesses, and trucks. The children's book industry has changed significantly in the past several decades. Take a look at a classic picture book like *The Story of Ferdinand* by Munro Leaf, for example. The story is very long, there are only a few colors, and the pictures are hard to see unless a child is sitting on a lap while reading. Contrast that with a more modern classic like *Pete the Cat: I Love My White Shoes* by Eric Litwin, and you will see what we mean. In this story, the text is written in a childlike way, there are very few words on each page, and the illustrations are bright and meaningful even to a room full of children observing from a distance. This is much more visually appealing to young children and more easily fosters print motivation.

- **Vocabulary:** Knowing the meaning of words, including names of things, feelings, concepts, and ideas. It also includes learning the meaning of new words (ECRR Chart).

Learning vocabulary is perhaps one of the most important and least fun parts of storytime. Reading books with repetition and pictures to go along with new words can help immensely with this process, as can singing songs with hand gestures or fingerplays. The Itsy Bitsy Spider, for example, climbs up a *waterspout*, which is a word that many children may not know. However, by singing the song, it can be implied that it is something vertical through which water falls when it rains and has an open bottom through which the spider can wash out. Children are much more likely to want to learn vocabulary when they are interested in the subject matter (like the dinosaur example mentioned earlier), but songs and rhymes are another great way to incorporate new vocabulary into the mix when subject matter alone is not enough.

- **Letter Knowledge:** Letters have names and represent sounds (ECRR Chart).

It goes without saying that knowledge and awareness of letters is a critical component of learning to read. But, often, letters are trickier than we realize! The same letter can look different in different books, with different fonts, or capitalized or in lowercase. Reading alphabet books can be a good start for building letter knowledge, especially when each page gets its own letter, and many books have been published to date that accomplish just that. However, projects at home and in the library can foster this knowledge even more. Drawing letters with a finger in applesauce, bubbles, or sand helps build the coordination necessary for writing later while simultaneously familiarizing children with each letter. Finger painting is another great way to build letters and juxtapose a tall "A" from a small "a." Letters can also be made by lining up pebbles or leaves on the ground, building the muscles that will one day hold a pencil in the process. Storytime can be an excellent place to initiate learning, but encouraging the continuation of that learning at home is even more valuable.

- **Print Awareness:** Knowing that print has meaning, how to handle a book, direction of print, author/title, and environmental print, all make up print awareness (ECRR Chart).

Print awareness can be built nearly anytime and anywhere. Encouraging caregivers to talk about the parts of a book and how a book is made helps children respect their books and understand them better. Even walking down the street, print is everywhere, from street signs to tags in the supermarket. Asking children to look out for a certain letter or word during the day can not only keep the child occupied on long trips in the car or the bus, but it also helps that child recognize print in the world and understand how important reading is to lifelong learning.

These six original concepts (though Narrative Skills and Print Motivation have now been combined) were thoroughly researched before, and studied after, implementation to observe their effects and to determine what was working and what was not. Librarians across the United States quickly began intentionally utilizing the six ECRR skills in their regularly scheduled storytime sessions, adding even more data to these studies. Our profession was enthusiastic about communicating to parents and caregivers the critical importance of storytime by demonstrating how storytimes were already covering the six ECRR targets, particularly narrative skills, vocabulary, phonological awareness, and print motivation (Neuman 1–77).

Though they were based on scientific research and clearly met the needs of young children, it was determined after a short time that the jargon of the six skills was too technical for many families to absorb easily. The original intention in quantifying these six targets was to enable and encourage families to continue working on these concepts at home. However, if the concepts were not easily understood, it was unlikely that they were being reinforced after storytime ended.

Observing the difficulty librarians and families were having with the technical nature of ECRR (now ECRR1), the project was revamped into what is known now as ECRR2, which translated the six early literacy skills into five more easily comprehensible and digestible practices. These practices still encompass the goals of ECRR1, but they are presented in ways that are easily accessible and understood by families and librarians alike. These five practices are: read, write, sing, talk, and play ("Building on Success").

- **Read:** Shared, or interactive, reading is the best way to build a child's interest in reading (ECRR Chart).

  This can be done in storytime, especially by reading books that have repetitive pieces that children can say along with the reader. At home, this can be replicated in a one-on-one setting as the reader asks the child questions as the book progresses.

- **Write:** Reading and writing both represent spoken language (ECRR Chart).

  This skill begins with the improvement of gross and fine motor skills. These skills can be practiced through fingerplays in storytime, weight-bearing activity on the hands like yoga for children (downward-facing dog), or even tummy time for littler ones. Grasping objects to move them from one place to another likewise builds these muscles and skills in a fun way.

- **Sing:** Singing utilizes rhyme, repetition, and cadence to slow down the sounds in words so that they are more easily heard and understood (ECRR Chart).

Singing can be a good way to introduce new vocabulary, as well. Though it can become tedious for both parents and storytime providers, repeating songs is one of the best ways children learn, particularly because repetition builds the neural pathways in the brain that were mentioned earlier. That is why a request for the alphabet song for the 20th time in a day should be met and celebrated!

- **Talk:** Talking in a way that encourages responses from children is essential (ECRR Chart).

This includes asking open-ended questions, telling and retelling stories, and talking about more than the here and now. These skills will later help children understand what they have read. This is part of where dialogic reading comes in: reading books with young children is not just about the text on the page, but it is also about making connections to a child's life outside the book and questions readers might develop as the story progresses.

- **Play:** Symbolic play, role-playing, and dramatic play all help strengthen language skills in young children (ECRR Chart).

Dramatizing a familiar story is a great example of play, whether it is through the use of puppets or one's own body. What might happen if the story were different? Encouraging play and reinforcing the fact that there are no right or wrong answers can help encourage independent thinking and creativity.

When ECRR2 was released, librarians had a much easier time communicating the newly condensed five practices to their storytime audiences, and families had a much easier time bringing those lessons home to their children. Storytimes are a way for libraries to regularly interact with children from the ages of zero to five and help prepare them for success in school by emphasizing these five practices during every storytime session.

ABOUT US

Hello, and welcome to our story. We are Kristin Grabarek and Mary R. Lanni, two librarians in the metropolitan Denver, Colorado, area who began implementing the ECRR skills and practices in our storytimes as soon as we stepped onto the storytime scene. We utilized the techniques that librarians across the United States were also using: reading books, encouraging interaction while reading, tying those books into songs and fingerplays, and linking those stories to take-home and other extension activities.

However, we soon began to realize that, though we were doing our best to include everyone who came to our storytime sessions, the main focus points of a traditional storytime were writing, singing, and talking, all centered on reading. These four of the five ECRR practices require some sort of shared language in order to be successful in a group setting. As the dynamics of our neighborhoods became more obvious, it was clear that English was not the only language being spoken in the homes of our attendees, and very often not the primary language being spoken. And this got us thinking.

Of the five practices, play is the only one that does *not* require a shared language to be successful in a group setting.

This means that, regardless of background or language, if a group learning activity was centered on play (as opposed to reading, writing, singing, or talking), families of all kinds could join together and participate in this activity. But is learning through play viable and justifiable?

LEARNING THROUGH PLAY

We were not the first to explore the importance of play-based learning. Think tanks, researchers, geniuses, and child influencers, among others, have long lauded the importance of play. Albert Einstein famously quipped, "Play is the highest form of research." In a more verbose comment, Fred Rogers remarked, "Play is often talked about as if it were a relief from serious learning. But for children, play is serious learning. Play is the work of childhood."

On a more serious note, the United Nations has even weighed in on the importance of play. Their 1989 Convention on the Rights of the Child determined play to be so important that it was included as a *basic right* of all children. The importance of this right was stated within the tragic contexts of child labor, war, violence, and poverty. Clearly, the right children have to play would be severely truncated if not eliminated in any of these horrific circumstances.

The American Academy of Pediatrics, however, finds that other children's right to play may also be truncated or undermined even in far less dire environments. Kenneth Ginsburg wrote in 2007 that "even those children who are fortunate enough to have abundant available resources and who live in relative peace may not be receiving the full benefits of play."

Ginsburg goes on to explain that highly scheduled lifestyles in which many children are raised, in the United States, limit the time children have for dramatic, organized, and free play. This, coupled with the more obvious limitations on play children facing poverty, abuse, and other toxic stressors experience, results in an urgent need to address the importance of play in children's social, emotional, and intellectual development as well as to provide more opportunities for children to play.

But, briefly, why exactly is play so important? Let us look again to the American Academy of Pediatrics for this answer. It outlines a lengthy list of the benefits of play, which include allowing children to develop and use creativity, to practice conflict resolution and problem solving, and to build confidence and self advocacy skills.

The American Academy of Pediatrics goes further to state that there are benefits of play for parents and caregivers, too, that go beyond those of raising creative, intelligent, resilient, and healthy children. Play allows parents to engage with the world from their child's point of view, which in turn improves parents' ability to communicate effectively with their children. On a simpler note, play allows parents an opportunity to engage with their children, which goes far to build lasting, quality relationships between parents and children.

Lastly, and just as important, play benefits the school learning environment as well. Again, from the American Academy of Pediatrics: play ensures that school learning is social and emotional as well as cognitive. Play, in a school setting, can also encourage children's ability to learn.

Despite the numerous benefits of play—and the fact that it is *fun!*—children in our society have experienced dramatically reduced opportunities for play. The National Association of Elementary School Principals tracked this reduction of playtime into children's kindergarten year. The association's decade-long study revealed at the start that almost all (96%) of participating kindergarten classrooms offered one or more recess periods per school day, defined as unstructured playtime. One decade later,

70 percent of kindergarten classrooms had only one recess period, and the remaining 30 percent of kindergarten classrooms had no unstructured playtime. Two years later, the well-intentioned No Child Left Behind Act solidified this trend by deliberately reducing time for recess and creativity to increase focus on reading and math.

Experts far more qualified than we are speculate on a number of unintended consequences of these decisions to reduce unstructured playtime in schools. While, yes, reading and math are of critical importance, in order to learn these skills, students must be able to focus on them. Removing outlets for physical and creative activity and exploration leaves learners in a sedentary environment that is not conducive to all learning styles. Children unable to learn in such an environment will not be able to succeed, even though they may be able to learn the exact same concepts in a more active, creative learning environment.

While this systemic conundrum far surpasses the influence of our play-based early learning programs in our respective libraries, it does serve to provide a larger perspective with regard to the importance of play in childhood development. At a minimum, our program moves play from being perceived as a break from learning to being seen as learning itself. Children, parents, caregivers, and supportive educators recognize the importance of play as the foundation of our early learning programs.

HOW PLAY SUPPORTS THE REST OF ECRR2

Play is both important and fun. Just as important, though, is the fact that play supports the four remaining ECRR2 practices.

- **Talk:** One of the tenets of talk in ECRR is to encourage families, the child's first and most important teacher, to teach by utilizing the language that is most comfortable for them. Even if this language is not the primary language spoken in the neighborhood or in the schools nearby, people are much better at explaining the world in their primary language than in a secondary one. Children are much better equipped for school when they learn concepts from their parents, regardless of the language through which they are learned. These concepts can be easily reinterpreted when utilizing the dominant language of the area, but they are difficult to learn in any language if not learned at all initially.

Programs that encourage learning through play allow families to be able to participate in their own language, working side by side with other families who may or may not share the same language. Though assimilation can weigh heavily on the minds of parents who may not speak the dominant language in their community, it is simply more important that children are learning as much as possible before attending school. The caregiver is the child's first and most important teacher, a fact that is reiterated both in this text and in our early learning programs. By receiving encouragement in a comfortable and supportive setting, parents of all backgrounds will feel more confident in their own ability to teach their young children and prepare them for success in school.

- **Sing:** Families can participate in a play-based activity, even if it does involve singing. Consider: how many readers of this work know *Frère Jacques* but are not fluent French speakers? Many of us would not know this tune had we been introduced to it with written lyrics we were unable to comprehend, but expected to sing aloud in front of our child and along with a group of fluent French speakers. However, through lighthearted practice and repetition, quite a few of us were able to learn this song and eventually pronounce the lyrics (mostly) correctly!

  A playful environment that includes clapping, dancing, and wiggling can easily encourage families to sing along, hum along, or clap along to an unfamiliar tune in an unfamiliar language. Again, placing play at the forefront of the learning experience invites families to engage immediately because it transcends barriers that a shared language implements. Plus, play is fun; everyone can have fun whether they are singing or not!

- **Write:** Families can engage in activities that prepare children to write in a learning environment centered on play. Consider common activities that build the fine motor skills needed to write successfully. Building block towers, threading colorful pasta onto yarn, and sculpting with clay or Play-Doh are among the first to come to mind. These activities, along with plenty of others, can be easily demonstrated to families without relying on any language at all. In fact, often enough, sitting a child down with blocks, pasta, yarn, clay, and Play-Doh will immediately result in his or her experimentation with these manipulatives without any adult guidance whatsoever. The child may even create a much more interesting way to play with these manipulatives than the traditional ways of interacting with them.

- **Read:** Perhaps this is the most difficult ECRR practice to incorporate into a play-based learning setting, but not an impossible one. Remember the importance of print motivation, the ECRR target defined by children being motivated to pick up a book. Including board books, pop-up books, and books with vivid pictures in a play-based learning environment gives books the role of toys rather than that of scholarly pursuits and places the language in which the book is written in a less important light (for now) than the book itself.

Recognizing how play can transcend barriers of language and culture while still supporting all five ECRR practices gave us confidence to explore the possibility of a play-based early learning program in our library settings. We recognized the importance of play and understood long-term benefits of play-based learning; however, we also saw potential immediate benefits of offering a play-based early learning program in a library setting.

PARTICIPANTS IN A TRADITIONAL STORYTIME

An immediate, key benefit of our play-based early learning programs was creating a space for families that may not attend a traditional storytime. While traditional storytimes are excellent and important library services, they may not feel comfortable, appear welcoming, or be accessible for some of the families in our communities. We certainly observed this to be the case in our respective libraries' communities and wanted to develop our play-based program in a way that intentionally included families that may find a traditional storytime out of bounds.

For the purposes of this discussion on families not often seen in traditional storytime settings, we will speak in broad strokes and make wide generalizations. The intention is not to cause offense, but rather to avoid doing so while still bringing to light the fact that storytimes reach some families more effectively than others. In order to avoid causing offense, we will limit these broad strokes and wide generalizations to our own library system. We trust that our readers will give us a small margin of error on some of our points as our library system is certainly not unique in terms of storytime attendance. Our intended purpose for this chapter is simply to convey our readers the importance of including all demographics in libraries' early learning offerings and to explain how a play-based early learning program will reach families that a traditional storytime may not or, in some ways, cannot.

Due to privacy concerns, libraries do not collect specific data about storytime attendees, thus making an empirical analysis of storytime participants impossible. However, we had the benefit of offering storytimes on a weekly basis over the course of several years and were therefore able to form a fairly comprehensive understanding of our regular storytime attendees.

To sum up bluntly: in our experience, traditional storytimes primarily benefit a specific type of families. Considering the typical participants in the storytimes we offered, we found these shared characteristics among them: many were mothers, some were nannies, and others were grandparents. Almost all spoke English as their primary language. Most appeared to be middle-income families, or at least not financially struggling families. All were able to attend a weekday, mid-morning program, many on a regular basis.

These observations over the course of several years gave us confidence that traditional storytimes were very effective in reaching particular demographics and not effective in reaching others. Furthermore, we observed that when our storytimes did draw a caregiver different from the profile drawn earlier, that caregiver appeared to be uncomfortable or unsure and he or she rarely returned. Let us take a moment to consider who does *not* regularly attend a traditional storytime.

- **Dads:** Finding a dad in a storytime is not unheard of, but it is less likely than finding a mom in a storytime. Given that dads are among the less frequent storytime attendees, it is understandable that they are sometimes uncomfortable participating, uncertain of how to participate, or reluctant to do so. And this is certainly understandable! Consider a roomful of sweet soprano voices singing along to "Baa Baa Black Sheep." When a tenor or bass voice joins in, it will stand out! And if that tenor or bass voice misses a word or skips to the wrong verse, it will be very clear which participant is not familiar with the lullaby lyrics. This alone lends to an understanding of why dads might hesitate before joining a storytime activity, or before joining a storytime at all.

- **Grandparents:** Grandparents, especially those who are infrequent caregivers, also face challenges when attending a modern traditional storytime. Storytimes of yesteryear required much more sitting, included much less singing, and rarely involved fingerplays or movement activities. These are the storytimes that existed when grandparents were parents attending with young children. Today's storytimes include very different books than grandparents may remember (consider *Ferdinand* versus *Pete the Cat,* as we previously mentioned), *plus* songs, fingerplays, and movement activities. For an infrequent caregiver with an expectation of a quiet reading event, this environment can be quite jarring.

- **Immigrant and Refugee Families:** Dads and grandparents, though, still benefit both from knowing the language being spoken during the storytime and from having a general cultural awareness of what norms and customs to expect of an American storytime audience. Immigrant and refugee families, including English language learners, not only face the challenges described earlier involving uncertainty with participation in a storytime but also lack the shared language and cultural understanding of the majority of traditional storytime attendees.

Each culture has its own traditions and expectations. One of the foundational tenets of the United States is that the country was created as a melting pot, a place where cultures the world over could come together and coexist, in its ideal state, harmoniously. An "American" culture has since been established, which often, as previously mentioned, targets a specific demographic of participant. Storytime is not excluded from this. Families from Latin cultures, for example, have a much stronger sense of family than many families from the prevailing American culture. This means that several generations may live in relatively close proximity to one another, and sometimes even in the same house.

This example of a strong family structure is the perfect learning environment for young children, especially as wisdom can be communicated among and within the generations. However, when Spanish may be the only language spoken with ease at home, attending a primarily English-speaking storytime with participants who may or may not speak Spanish themselves can be disconcerting.

Regardless of the cultural norms, attending any program, particularly storytime, when it is unpredictable or unfamiliar, is understandably difficult. Thus, by creating programming that fosters learning outside the storytime landscape can provide a platform for a new cultural norm to develop, even if it exists only within the confines of those programs.

- **Wiggly Children:** Storytimes require a lot of coordinated action from participants. If you are a grown-up participant, the expectations of a traditional storytime are well within the realm of possibility. If you are a three-year-old participant, the chances of success decrease significantly. Of course, storytime providers are very used to this and allow for mishaps and disruptions. That said, while many children obviously enjoy the storytime environment, its structure is simply not suited to all children.

  Some children need a more active environment in which they can learn. They may want to take a shorter or longer time with a movement activity or fingerplay, sing another verse of the song, dance instead of sing, or simply not sit. Traditional storytimes, however, rely on at least a semblance of structure in order to be successful. A storytime needs to, for example, include a story. A child who simply cannot sit and listen to a story is no less capable of learning than a child who can, but *does* need a different learning environment, both to allow him or her to learn successfully and to avoid detracting from the learning experience of the sitters and listeners.

- **Children with Special Needs:** Varying learning needs are even more significant and pronounced for our children who are differently abled or who struggle with sensory processing. If a child needs calm and quiet or, conversely, to be constantly on the move in order to focus and learn, traditional storytime may not be the ideal environment for that child. More and more, storytime providers are taking these needs into consideration, but they usually take place in a storytime setting created specifically for these learners instead of being incorporated into a regularly scheduled storytime event.

- **Affluent Parents:** Some parents believe that traditional storytimes are simply not relevant to their families. Parents who can afford other learning opportunities for their children may choose to enroll in those rather than attend a library storytime. Mommy-and-me classes such as music, creative movement, yoga, and art are quite popular in our society and reach a specific demographic that is able to afford them. These parents may see traditional storytimes as too simplistic for their families' needs compared to experiences these classes provide. Also, for many of these parents, when something is provided free of charge, its value is comparably negated.

- **Engaged Parents:** Parents who regularly read to their children and are actively participating in their learning may not see a storytime as a valid activity to attend, as it appears to duplicate their efforts at home.

- **Working Parents:** Still other parents may simply experience scheduling conflicts with a traditional storytime. Storytimes tend to be offered on weekday mornings, when working parents are often otherwise occupied and stay-at-home parents may be engaged in one of the aforementioned activities. It is not possible to attend every learning opportunity available in a community, and some parents may place a storytime lower on their list of priorities than either necessary or more preferable activities.

Additionally, some caregivers work more than the standard 40-hour workweek, especially those with lower-paying jobs. The schedules of these jobs can vary widely, and even if a caregiver is not scheduled to be at work during a storytime session, he or she may simply be too tired to bring the child to storytime.

IN DEFENSE OF STORYTIMES

It is imperative to us that we emphasize this critical point before continuing this discussion: in both of our library settings, our play-based learning programs exist *alongside* our traditional storytime programs. Indeed, our goal has never been, nor will it ever be, *to replace* a traditional storytime program with a new early learning program model.

We firmly believe there is a place for both programs in the library setting, and more importantly a *need* for both; as we discussed previously, play does support the four remaining ECRR practices. However, of the four, it supports reading the least. All five ECRR practices are critical to early learning. Our program model places play at the center and uses that to support singing, talking, and writing. A traditional storytime places reading at the center and also uses that to support singing, talking, and writing. We truly believe our play-based learning program works best in tandem with a traditional storytime: one catches families most comfortable with learning through play, and the other reaches families able to learn through reading.

A PLAY-BASED LEARNING ALTERNATIVE

Our play-based learning model welcomes caregivers that traditional storytimes miss in a number of ways. Primarily, our programs offer learning experiences that do not require a shared language to enjoy. Families are able to talk through the play-based activities in whatever language is most comfortable to them. Immigrant and refugee families need not speak English or be familiar with storytime structure to participate and enjoy play-based activities.

Furthermore, since the learning process is based on play, caregivers with a traditionally more "fun" role (i.e., grandparents and infrequent caregivers) can laugh, experiment, crack jokes, and so forth throughout the process; a play-based learning experience is less rigid and formal than traditional storytimes tend to be.

Finally, families that may see storytime as redundant or simplistic will find value in these play-based activities. Parents can expose their early learners to a variety of opportunities through this program series while learning how these activities develop skills needed for school readiness and success.

Continuing through this text, we will share our ideas and methods for creating programs with a budget of any size and how to utilize community members to enhance the early learning experience.

IN SUMMARY

It is our hope that this text is useful across the spectrum of individuals who work with children in this age group and their families. From librarians to child care providers, from those already versed on the importance of learning between the ages of zero and five to those to whom some of this information may be new. At the end of each chapter, you will find a section like this, entitled "In Summary." Here will be a synopsis of the chapter for a quick review of the major topics of discussion. While it is our intention that the bulk of the chapter is both useful and well synthesized, we also understand the time constraints of those in these very important positions. So, we ask that you read what you can when you can, incorporating these ideas into your work to improve the education of our society and the children who reside here.

- Every Child Ready to Read (ECRR2) was developed by and for librarians to encourage the education of children and their families through storytime. Its main concepts–read, write, sing, talk, and play–encourage reading skills from the beginning with the goal of inspiring children to not only learn to read but to enjoy doing so. Reading on grade level at third grade sets children up for success for the rest of their education and their lives.

- For the purposes of our book, play is the target ECRR practice. Our library programming focuses on this concept, as it is the one that does not require a shared language and can thus serve communities of various nationalities and primary languages. Play builds life skills, cooperation, and gross and fine motor function in a fun, creative space.

- Storytime is still a critical component of library function and children's education. What we are advocating here is a complement to storytime: while storytime requires shared language, our programs do not. However, a combination of the two prepares children to not only understand language and the components of it, but also how these ideas play out in the real world.

- Through our experiences and observations, we have determined that a play-based learning alternative gets families learning together and encourages the continuation of this shared learning after the library event has ended. These activities keep families returning to the library again and again, building confidence and camaraderie with each repeat visit.

TWO

Creating an Early Learning Program Series

ORIGINAL CREATION OF PLAY-BASED EARLY LEARNING PROGRAMS

We began brainstorming play-based programs for families at approximately the same time, independently of one another and on opposite sides of the city of Denver. Both of our libraries conducted regular storytimes during the week with good attendance, but it had become obvious to both of us that there were families we would see outside of the library in the neighborhood or simply outside of storytime who were unfamiliar to us. Though these families would benefit from attending storytimes, for various reasons, storytime in its usual format was not the right approach. Both of our communities clearly needed an alternative to traditional storytime programming in order to reach all the families with young children our library branches served.

Little University: A Note on Kristin's Library Community

Kristin's branch library is situated in a curious location. The neighborhoods nearest the library are made up largely of new-ish two-story homes occupied by middle- to upper-middle-class, white, college-educated parents and their children. However, just beyond these neighborhoods are apartment complexes and lower-income housing that is serving as a much-needed refuge for a great many African and Middle-Eastern immigrant and refugee families. These communities both find exceptional value in their local branch library and take full advantage of its materials, resources, and programming.

This branch library has a successful history with traditional storytimes and offers three storytime sessions each week for babies, toddlers, and preschoolers. Sessions are consistently and enthusiastically attended by the young children of the branch's white, college-educated neighbors, brought by either their mothers or nannies.

After working in this library location a handful of months and experimenting with a fourth, all-ages, storytime to see if it might draw new or different storytime attendees (it did not), Kristin began to take note of two separate facts simultaneously: first, that immigrant and refugee families were certainly utilizing the library and attending library programming but were conspicuously absent during storytime sessions despite the number of very young children in these families; and second, that a number of families with young children utilized the library on weekends for materials but were uninterested in attending the weekday storytime sessions. As a parent of a young child herself, Kristin was able to casually chat with these families and surmise that while they were seeking some early learning opportunities, they did not find library storytimes relevant to their needs.

Kristin began to consider what early learning programming might look like that could meet both the articulated early learning interests of the affluent families and the presumed early learning interests of the immigrant and refugee families in her community. As discussed in the previous chapter, the successful program formula seemed to center on one tenet: *play*. Kristin believed that immigrant and refugee families were not attending traditional storytimes because the format itself did not appeal to them. The need for a shared language, some level of cultural awareness, and the days and times storytime was scheduled, together, were not able to effectively connect with these families. At the same time, Kristin believed that affluent families felt storytimes to be redundant to the activities they were already involving their children in elsewhere and at home.

With the support of her supervisor and branch manager, Kristin put together a year-long plan for an early learning program series called Little University. The initial sketch of this program series outlined weekly, half-hour sessions delivered every Saturday, mid-morning. Every program in the series focused on some aspect of early learning that did not require a book or the English language to convey. Most programs in the series included activities that promoted fine motor skill development, rhythm and movement, science and nature, and wellness. Each program intentionally targeted one social-emotional learning opportunity, as well, even if that opportunity was merely taking turns.

Kristin had no budget, no program precedent, and no idea if this would work. She relied heavily on conversations with and, even more heavily, on her observations of program participants to gauge the effectiveness of these programs. Were the attendees smiling? Were they comfortable? Or were they confused, nervous, and weirded out? Were only the English speakers clear as to what to do, or was everyone able to participate? Were parents with babies as engaged as parents with preschoolers? Did the families leave feeling as though their experience had been a success? Did the families return?

As the year progressed, Kristin invited cultural institutions and local business owners already working with young children to deliver one of their early learning opportunities as part of her program series. The Colorado Ballet facilitated a Creative Movement class where the children rotated through various animal-based dances. A local yoga teacher brought a picture book to life with simple yoga poses children and caregivers could attempt together and laughed along with them when those poses did—or did not—go as planned. A shop owner brought over an array of essential oils and allowed the children to mix bubble baths and room spritzers while parents learned the various essential oil properties. The Denver Zoo brought three live animals, one of which the children could touch (the python)! An author came and read his children's book aloud and then taught all the children and parents how to draw his main character.

The weekends an outside presenter was not available, Kristin and the Little University families made bird feeders out of toilet paper tubes, constructed terrariums from plants donated from a local greenhouse and jars and dirt collected from community members, made Play-Doh from a Pinterest recipe with basic kitchen ingredients, constructed glittery calming jars from supplies left over from a teen event at the branch, painted with their fingers, made buildings out of donated Legos and toys, and fashioned Dr. Seuss-esque gardens out of unwanted pipe cleaners, pony beads, and modeling clay.

Week after week, the families kept returning. The non-English-speaking families cautiously experimented with the materials provided. The dads made dad jokes (especially about the python). The grandparents took pictures. Several caregivers offered to write letters of support for the program series. Several immigrant families arrived subsequent weeks with friends in tow. Children became more outgoing, parents started to offer anecdotes of how the programs had positively affected their child's development, and everyone began asking for the schedule for the following week, then the following month.

Cultural institutions and local business owners began to inquire about future opportunities to present new programs and how to make donations to existing programs.

By the fall—appropriately timed right as a new school year began—Little University programs were established. The community embraced them with excitement and enthusiasm, and quite possibly with pride, and the series was quickly seen as a key part of the branch library's program offerings.

Family Literacy: A Note on Mary's Library Community

The neighborhood surrounding Mary's particular library branch is markedly different from that surrounding Kristin's. It is a neighborhood that is rapidly gentrifying, with homes that have been in existence for decades juxtaposed against plots that had been demolished and rebuilt within the last few years. Likewise, the community itself is a mixture of people who have lived in the area for generations and those who are new to it, with a strong majority of library users being of Mexican descent.

Storytime tended to see more of the upper-class, white community that surrounded the library, but the library is frequented at other times by the Latino community. Rarely did the two interact in the library, much less in library programs, even though they were neighbors.

Mary and her then supervisor sat down and examined the demographics of their library users, including the things that were familiar and desired by those users. One of the main considerations was that families of Mexican descent in the area often lived either with several generations under one roof or with extended family members nearby. Family was of paramount importance to this group, and they wanted to reflect that importance in library programming.

As these events began to take off in both locations, Kristin and Mary realized that they had been working on the same trajectory and discussed the possibility of joining forces to make the program even stronger and more streamlined.

At the time, Mary and her then supervisor determined that the term Little University, which Kristin was already using, was perhaps not the best fit for the families in their neighborhood. Their concern was that the term "University" might feel off-putting or irrelevant to families who may not have attended a university themselves, which was the case for many of the families in their service area.

Instead, they elected to use the title "Family Literacy" for their early learning program series, to encourage familial participation both within and outside of the library branch and to honor the fact that many of their library users placed premium value on families engaging in events and activities together. These programs were not just designed for children with caregivers sitting on the outside of what was happening; families were encouraged to participate and learn together.

Just as with Kristin's branch, Saturdays were the most convenient programming day for families in Mary's community. Whether they worked steady or variable jobs, many families from across the spectrum were available that day. However, maintaining consistency in these programs was challenging at Mary's branch because her schedule had her on rotating weekends, meaning that she was at the library only every other Saturday and not all of her other staff members were comfortable presenting this program. This is why it is so important to have staff buy-in when starting programs like these. Because families do better with regular and predictable programming, it was critical that a solution be reached in order for the program to be successful. This spurred the necessity for several conversations and considerations as the program was getting off the ground.

After many of these discussions and budgetary review, it was determined that inexpensive, local presenters would help to satisfy the programming needs of the library on the Saturdays when Mary was not scheduled to work. This allowed other staff to supervise the program without having to facilitate it. They were lucky to find two presenters to teach yoga and Zumbini (an early literacy–based Zumba program), which satisfied all of their needs initially. An additional component to the Zumbini program was that it was able to be presented bilingually in English and Spanish to meet the needs of the Spanish-speaking community that Mary was hoping to reach.

Yoga and Zumbini programs were selected purposefully based on the needs of the community surrounding the library. First, both programs require bodily movement and engagement to be successful. In the Latino community, among others, obesity is of major concern. Though there are many factors contributing to this epidemic, it was thought that by having healthy movement programs offered regularly, families could be introduced to healthy living practices together that they would then take home and continue.

Second, chronic stress is one of the most powerful reasons why some children struggle to succeed in school. Much of this stress can stem from not having healthy outlets when life at home is a struggle. A child's basic food, living, and safety needs must be met in order for learning and growth to occur. Yoga helps mitigate this by teaching self-soothing techniques, focusing inward, and finding patience. Zumbini encourages movement to music, which releases endorphins and helps improve mood and focus.

Though these programming goals may seem outside of the scope of a library's mission, we argue that on the contrary, they are directly in line with it. A library is one of the last public places families can go to learn for free, and it is therefore the responsibility of the library to provide opportunities to educate the public in all faculties. By providing programs such as yoga and Zumbini, libraries improve the quality of a library user's mental state to encourage further learning and success both in school and in life. This success, then, permits library users to further pursue the goals that are important to them and make the community more robust and healthy.

The Saturday programs drew in a blend of the families living in Mary's service area: both those who had been in the neighborhood for generations and those who had newly arrived, including families of various cultural backgrounds. In one place, they were introduced to one another in a way that observed and celebrated their similarities, while their differences mattered little. The programs that were delivered on these Saturdays included primarily yoga and Zumbini, both of which utilize the body to experience movement and tranquility. Whether or not participants had previous experience with these activities was not important; everyone entered the room prepared to learn and interact, and each event was well received. (Bringing in paid presenters can, however, become expensive and limiting, especially to small branches or library systems with small budgets. Never fear! More on working within small budgets will be discussed in Chapter 4.)

After nearly a year of work on the Family Literacy program, Mary received a promotion and transitioned to a small neighborhood library nearer to central downtown. Interestingly, one of the neighborhoods she served in her previous library was between the two libraries, meaning that some of her customers overlapped. However, the two branches themselves could not have felt more different. The implications of this important fact will be discussed in more detail next.

CONSIDERATIONS FOR CREATING PLAY-BASED PROGRAMS IN YOUR LIBRARY

Cultural Awareness

In order to ensure that library programming is designed to meet the needs of all intended targets, it is important to be familiar with the community surrounding the library and any cultural norms that exist within that community.

As an example, remember Mary's initial library branch: located on the western side of Denver, in a neighborhood that housed a large population of Spanish-speaking families, many of whom had lived in the area for generations. At the time Mary was considering her early learning programming plan, this area was rapidly gentrifying. Mary observed a dichotomy of library usage that mirrored the two populations living in her library branch's neighborhood: while the majority of the people using library materials and its facilities were those who had been in the neighborhood for much longer, most of the people who were attending weekly storytimes were the families new to the area, not those who spoke Spanish but rather those who spoke English and fit the more "traditional" storytime participant mold as discussed in the Introduction.

Mary then began looking to the Spanish-speaking families themselves—those not attending storytimes but nonetheless utilizing the library regularly—attempting to determine not only what type of library program would be most beneficial to them but also when that sort of program should be offered. Realizing her own lack of knowledge on the matter as a whole, Mary found beginning conversations with these families was not only humbling but helped her build connections with them.

These relationships would plant the seeds for further participation in library programming for library users of all ages.

Regardless of your own cultural background—or perhaps using that as a stepping stone—it is imperative to begin any new library programming venture by first building awareness of, sensitivity to, and acceptance of all cultures, specifically those surrounding your library location. You can always start by reading, but meeting and building positive relationships with people can usually provide more insight. Once you learn some of the key components of the cultures frequenting your library, use those as guides for creating programs that are meaningful to your library community.

Marketing

Once you have a program idea in place and an awareness of how this idea meets the needs and interests of your library's constituents, the next important consideration is how you will fill your space and make your time and money worthwhile. Your library likely has several marketing options at its disposal: print calendars, Facebook events, Twitter, regular newsletters, flyers, word of mouth, event listings on the library's website, and signs in the library, just to name a few. Which of these tools will be most successful in your community is up to you to determine. Trial and error is all a part of the process! For an example of these materials, please see Appendix C.

Trust is a core component of encouraging program participation, particularly for those families who may not always feel comfortable in a library program setting. Word of mouth, flyers, and Facebook promotion all target library users in different ways, and the users who respond to each type of marketing differ.

Word of Mouth

Word of mouth may seem tedious or insubstantial, but it can truly be the strongest marketing tool a library can utilize to encourage attendance at library programs, regardless of the user's background. Consider your own likelihood of attending events based on whether you are personally invited, invited to attend with someone you already know, or saw the event advertised on a flyer or online. A personal invitation, or an invitation to attend with a friend, begins your process of attending with ease and comfort. The uncertainty of entering a new space and an unfamiliar event is greatly offset by the comfort of knowing that you will be greeted personally, or that you will have someone with you that you know. Building relationships with library users and encouraging them to build relationships with each other will go far to fill your program with comfortable, interested attendees.

We will use Kristin's library setting as an example for this point. The demographics in Kristin's neighborhood were such that word of mouth was already a very dynamic component among the populations in her neighborhood. Many moms in more-affluent families utilized word of mouth through playdates, mommy group meet-ups, and morning coffee dates. Very similarly, immigrant and refugee families relied heavily on each other for information. Meeting to share childcare, to chat with neighbors, or to welcome extended family members for meals provided opportunities to share information regarding events within the community. In these instances, word of mouth was even more important, as a great many promotional materials simply could not be translated into the varied languages spoken in our immigrant and refugee communities.

To emphasize this important point further: word of mouth is not only about library users telling other library users about an upcoming program or event. This process starts with library users experiencing quality programming that they *want* to tell others about; an occurrence which, in turn, starts with librarians *creating* quality programming for these library users to experience. Getting a high-quality program off the ground is very much a chicken-or-egg experience when it comes to marketing.

This marketing still involves those librarians *talking* to their library users both inside and outside of the library to make sure they are aware of and interested in the programs being offered. After each program, it is useful to continue this word-of-mouth process by getting feedback from those participants to see what can be changed or improved for the next program; informally, this can be done by simply chatting with the attendees after the program. It seemed that for every one family Kristin communicated with, two or three additional families were being reached by word of mouth.

For introverted librarians, the word-of-mouth marketing can be quite a challenge! What we have found that can help is having something in hand and an elevator speech to start. It is much easier to talk about something that excites you, so if you can determine what that might be, it makes a difference. For some ideas of elevator speeches to get you started, please see Appendix A.

It may come as a relief now to note that librarians are not solely responsible for this marketing task; rather, every person on the library's staff should be familiar with the programs and encouraged to begin these conversations with library users. This presents a united front on the part of the library and helps families feel welcome no matter who might be on the schedule at a particular day or time.

Getting to know the families frequenting the library, particularly those who would come in outside of normal storytime hours, and inviting them to the new early learning programs literally built the attendance in both of our programs. Not only that, but it meant that when those families did arrive, there was already an established rapport between them and the library staff that helped put them at ease in a situation that might be new or unfamiliar.

Print Collateral

In addition to word-of-mouth marketing, it can be helpful to have some kind of print collateral for those families who like to have calendars up on their refrigerators as reminders of goings on in the community. Together with the marketing department, Kristin developed a logo for Little University that is on all Little University marketing materials. Having something that is tangible, recognizable, and consistent increases the professionalism of a program and the library itself. If you do not have access to someone who can create logos for you within your library, consider asking for volunteers from the community who might have skills with logos or other design work. One of the many benefits of working in a library is that the library is one of the places that people are most willing to assist for free.

Having calendars available at each program, and making sure that people know that you have them, is another invitation for a conversation. It is good to have the current month and the following month on hand if you can, because once people get hooked, they will want the newest edition as soon as it is available.

Following Up

So, people are starting to show up for your new program. That's excellent! One quick, helpful thing to do, after thanking them for coming of course, is to learn where they found out about the program—another nightmare for an introverted librarian, but an incredibly important component to future program success. An example from one of Mary's programs came from a mom and daughter who had never visited any library location before. When asked, they said that they learned about Mary's early learning program from a Mommy Facebook page. This was a surprise as it was not one of the places where Mary had marketed her program! How it had gotten there was a mystery, but this much is true: families in a close-knit neighborhood are not independent silos. They have webs of communication that may be invisible to those working in a library who never see the families at all or never see them together. This means that building positive relationships with one family spreads those emotions in a web from one to the next, bringing them together at what is quickly becoming one of the last free community-gathering places in a city setting: the library.

Scheduling

After talking with customers and evaluating the library's existing programming schedule, Saturday mornings came out as the most popular and convenient time for families to attend early learning programs at the library in both of our locations. We focused on this time to allow working families the chance to attend a library program with their children outside the rigid confines of the traditional workday. As you are evaluating your own program, you may determine that another day or time works better for your community. Whatever seems to be the most successful option is just fine!

We determined that the Saturday mid-morning time slot was best in terms of scheduling via a handful of methods, some labor intensive and some simply observational. One immediate hint was noting that even though no programming was being offered at this day and time, families with young children were regularly utilizing the library on Saturday mid-mornings, anyway.

As far as the more labor-intensive approach, Kristin made online and in-person inquiries to determine if any programming was available in her neighborhood on Saturday mornings and, if so, what programming it was. (Answer: Soccer for toddlers, preschoolers, and kids during some months, and a handful of classes at local rec centers that unfortunately often went wait-listed. No free programming was available that Kristin found.)

At the same time, both of us had quick, simple conversations with the families in our libraries: "If we were to begin offering early learning programs, what day and time do you think would work best to have them?" Or, "if there were a parent-child dance class on a Saturday morning, would your family be able to come to that? If not, would there be a better time for me to offer it?"

These conversations were beautiful in their simplicity for a number of reasons. One, it gave us yet another opportunity for the important word-of-mouth marketing we mentioned earlier. Two, it gave our families a sense of ownership over the program: they could provide feedback, share ideas, and/or express enthusiasm and support. For example, a number of parents

Kristin communicated with provided even more information than what Kristin was seeking: parents lamented a lack of early learning or weekend program offerings in the neighborhood and an interest in trying things like this programming but having difficulty finding a time or location in which to do so. And, most importantly, these quick conversations opened the door for follow-up conversations: "Hi, I got that program we were talking about booked for this coming Saturday! Would you like a schedule of everything we have going on this month?" This is a much easier interaction to have than trying to hand a schedule or flyer to someone who has no knowledge or context for your conversation.

Scheduling, however, will always be tricky. One of the most frustrating parts of scheduling programming for children of ages zero through five is the nap schedule. Naps are always hard to work around when planning programs for this age group. Not only are they constantly changing, but each child has different needs and it is impossible to find a time that works for every child all the time. As long as you can find some sort of critical mass, that will do just fine. The families who can attend at any given point may fluctuate, but they will be able to keep the schedule in the back of their minds for when their routine permits them to attend.

After examining all the complex and commonsense information we had gleaned in terms of scheduling, we then considered one final bit of information: traditional program scheduling in our library branches and throughout our library system. We looked specifically at the timing of other children's programming during the week. Since regular weekly storytimes were scheduled at 10:30 a.m. and had good attendance, we decided that Saturday programs should also to be offered at that time not only because it seemed to be a universally convenient time for families, but also to maintain consistency in the early learning programming in our libraries.

Building a Core Group of Participants

As any storytime provider or library program coordinator can tell you, having a core group of participants at each program is critical to the success of that program. These families, even if not all of them attend every session, are those who support the program's mission and are already comfortable with the structure and the expected behavior and outcomes of the program.

New families will look to these core attendees as guides for them and their children as they navigate their way through the program. These families will naturally become friends and encourage regular attendance. If you have ever gone to a fitness class at the gym, you know that you can immediately pick out the people who are there for every single class because they are doing exactly what the instructor asks and can serve as models as the class progresses. Likewise, if you get to know someone in the class or, even better, the teacher as well, you will have more motivation to return again and again.

Like your class at the gym, you know that early literacy programs are most beneficial when attended regularly. Your library users know that, too. So, building relationships with those families and among those families will ensure repeat attendance and, therefore, your program's continued success.

How, though, can you build those relationships? One way is to find common ground with your participants. If you have children, talk about them and their learning path. If you come from a similar cultural background, use that as a foundation. As you get to know your participants more, you will learn more about them. These details can help you build bridges between new families and those more established in the program, encouraging them to communicate with one another even more than with you.

HOW TO STRUCTURE THE PROGRAM SERIES

There are several different goals of the Little University early learning programming model. We believe it is important to incorporate art, movement, and STEM regularly into the programming schedule. The program series is ultimately about preparing children from birth through preschool for kindergarten readiness and success. A number of objectives must be met in order for a child to be both ready for, and successful in, kindergarten. These include improving gross and fine motor skills, letter and number knowledge, shape and color recognition, and vocabulary and print awareness. Children must also practice basic communication and social skills such as asking for and using the restroom, being able to take turns and share, and basic self-control.

It truly takes a village to expose young children to these learning opportunities and to do so with enough regularity that they are confidently prepared for kindergarten. Luckily, our library communities are surrounded by just such a village!

We looked initially to our own expertise and experience to develop these learning experiences for our program series. Ample opportunities exist for librarians to put together art, movement, STEM, and other early learning programming themselves to build kindergarten readiness skills. But we both recognized that even greater experiences could be provided to families by bringing in other program presenters as a part of their program series.

Starting out, we only had a handful of program presenters and program options outside the library from which to choose: the oft-thought of cultural institutions like the zoo or science museum, and baby-toddler-preschooler mommy-and-me classes. Reaching out and connecting with these local organizations proved to be the easiest and most effective way of building the core set of early learning opportunities for the program series. (It is worth noting that in doing this outreach, the library is not only able to partner with others for a very effective early learning program series, but doing so also establishes relationships that can continue into other programming and event capacities.)

The two following chapters will outline in detail the core early learning programs that make up the series, along with the programs that have been developed from this core series since the program's inception. Chapter 3 is devoted to working with a programming budget, and Chapter 4 describes early learning programs that require minimal, if any, funding.

Regardless of your library's budget, each of several important touchstones should be attempted every month at best, or at least every quarter. It is also recommended that this program continue year-round without any breaks in order to encourage repeat attendance and the momentum of the program series itself. When people know to expect something fun and exciting at the library every Saturday, they are exponentially more likely to return. If, however, they are under the impression that something exciting happens every Saturday and they arrive one week and something is not happening, that can stop the forward momentum and perhaps even prevent the return of that family.

These are the target areas for programming in a regular cycle for this program:

Movement

- These types of programs are critical for improving gross motor skills (which, in turn, promote the improvement of fine motor skills for future writing ability).

- Yoga, dance, and soccer are only a few of the many possibilities for movement-based programming in the library. Depending on the space available (inside or outside of the library), some programs may be more appropriate for your location than others.

STEM (Science, Technology, Engineering, Math)

- STEM is another important buzzword in the library and educational communities. The more exposure children have to programming of this type from a young age, the more likely they are to pursue it or, at the very least, understand it as they continue through school. Even if children do not have an interest in a STEM-related career, they will be expected to take coursework pertaining to it up to college entrance exams at least. STEM programming from an early age will ensure that these difficult concepts are attainable and understandable.

- Counting games, animal presentations, basic science experiments, and investigating the properties of various substances all fall under this important umbrella. One of the most valuable components of library programming is that these programs go from being intimidating to being *fun* for both the children and *the caregivers*, encouraging further exploration at home.

Art

- As arts programs are disappearing from schools nationwide due to budget cuts and other prioritization, it is even more critical that art is available to children and families in libraries. It should be emphasized here as in all other programming—*especially for children*—that these experiences are about the *process* and not the *product*.

- Regardless of the presenter's own ability and knowledge, art can be expressed in myriad ways. From paper collages to clay sculptures to paintings, a variety of budgetary levels are possible, as well. As children use their fingers to create designs in paint or to place paper or other objects in a collage, they are enhancing their fine motor skills in a safe and nonjudgmental environment. Even better for parents, they do not have to worry about getting paint all over their house in the process!

Health and Nutrition

- Healthful eating and movement are critical at all stages of life, and depending on familial background or income level, there may or may not be much exposure to this kind of lifestyle. By inviting programming that emphasizes the importance of healthy behavior in a way that is accessible with regard to both time required and financial obligation, it is more likely to be replicated outside of the library.

- Programs where children prepare food for themselves give them a sense of pride and independence, especially when they are able to then deliver the finished product to their parents directly. Being able to slice, mix, and scoop means that children are building important musculature that will in turn prepare them for writing. Parents may not expect that their children will be able to perform the tasks asked of them in these programs; by watching them do so, however, parents are learning ways to empower their children at home while the children are also improving the muscle control necessary to support those tasks.

Wellness

- Kindness, empathy, self-control, and self-awareness are becoming increasingly touted as important social-emotional skills to practice prior to entering kindergarten. Programs that allow children an opportunity to interact, communicate, and experience the processes of waiting and listening are critical experiences to set children up for success in kindergarten.

- Yoga, meditation, and aromatherapy may seem like far-off concepts for this age group, but they are, in fact, prime opportunities for children to learn self-regulation techniques that will prepare them for the nervousness, anxiety, and uncertainty they will likely experience when entering kindergarten.

- Furthermore, many families that utilize the library come from unpleasant and, at times, dire circumstances. Community or domestic violence, poverty, and stressors related to immigration are among the challenges many of our young children face; wellness programming equips them with tools and strategies to help manage the big feelings that come with difficult experiences.

By having an established core for your library's early learning programming, you are making it easier to schedule the program series because you are focusing on a specific formula while planning. Additionally, families like structure and predictability, especially if they miss a program, because they know that there will be other opportunities to improve those skills in future sessions.

It is important to note here that repetition of a presenter or program is not only allowed, but it is encouraged. Like in storytime when songs are repeated over and over to reinforce them in a child's brain, so too are neural connections reinforced by repeating activities. As mentioned earlier, if a family misses one of a particular program, there will be other opportunities to attend at another time. However, if a family does come to, say, a yoga program several times, both the caregivers and the library staff will see improvement in the child's abilities from one session to the next. This can help support the program from a grant writer's perspective, as well!

Additionally, depending on the support a library has for this programming, especially if grants or other entities require some sort of tangible data, being able to track progress may be critical. Developing a predictable and intentional schedule of programming with desired goals helps make this process easier.

HOW THE PROGRAM SUPPORTS SOCIAL-EMOTIONAL SKILLS

In order to be successful in school, children between the ages of zero and five must learn several important skills, including self-regulation, patience, sharing, and kindness. Though this may seem outside of the scope of the library's goals, particularly in the fact that nowhere in those skills can reading or writing be found, it does in fact fall into the consideration of "early learning."

We mentioned yoga earlier and will start with this to illustrate this point. Yoga teaches patience and self-control through its blend of deep breathing and held poses. Though children may not close their eyes or remain completely still, they are absorbing the quiet and the teachings of yoga and are learning self-regulatory techniques along the way. Children, regardless of background, often find comfort on the space of their mat. The mat can represent physical space that belongs only to them, on which they are safe. Through yoga, they can focus on themselves and on their own movement instead of comparing themselves to others or judging others' successes and failures. Reminding them of this quiet, safe space can help regulate behavior and calm children off the mat, as well, lowering the levels of cortisol in their brain and allowing them to think, and then to learn, more easily.

Art programs are another excellent example to consider. Art primarily encourages creative expression through color and shapes. But even more subtle social-emotional learning opportunities exist with art programs.

When materials are set out before the program begins and participants are expected to patiently wait for instructions before starting, they are learning self-regulation skills that will be important in school. They understand that they will be able to participate in the program, but that there is a structure that they must respect before being able to do so.

Movement programs, like those relating to dance, are yet another example of an opportunity to develop social-emotional skills. Dance programs encourage self-expression, raise endorphin levels, and build strength and cardiovascular endurance. This fun activity is one that can be easily replicated at home, as well, and is beneficial for both adults and children alike. Dancing to a favorite song releases feel-good endorphins that can help with mood regulation and increase focus, skills that children will need when they find themselves in school at no matter what age. Sometimes, taking a quick dance or movement break can mean the difference between having a meltdown and solving a challenging problem.

THE IMPORTANCE OF LEARNING TOGETHER

As families learn together through the many activities provided through play-based programming at the library, children and caregivers alike are learning ways to cope with nervousness and uncertainty, communicating with one another, and building bonds and confidence that will endure beyond the class itself. The stronger the familial support system, the more successful a child will be in school and in life. Libraries are some of the few remaining neighborhood gathering spots and are therefore emboldened to provide space where families are not only reading together, but are preparing for success in every aspect of their lives. Early learning programming provides many of these tools for success, on a consistent basis, and in a safe and welcoming environment.

ONE LAST NOTE

In this chapter, we described in detail our unique library communities, highlighting the differences between families within each community and the differences between the communities themselves. Take note, though, that the early learning program series developed for these two communities were far more similar than different; in fact, on paper both early learning program series look almost identical.

Mary had a valuable career opportunity arise after developing her initial Family Literacy early learning program series, which included a transfer to a different branch library. This branch library community was different from both Kristin's and from the one in which Mary originally worked.

One of the challenges at Mary's new library was the fact that it lacked any sort of private space where storytime or other program could occur without disrupting the rest of the library users. This meant that, although there had been a regular storytime, there had not been other programming for children beyond that. As Mary began settling into her job there, she began to notice two things: first, that there were a lot (a *lot!*) of young children and new families in the neighborhood, and second, that those families were itching to have children's programming in their library. Because of its central location, free parking, and willing participants, it was an ideal location to continue the play-based programming that she had been presenting at her previous library. This time, however, the audience and the playing field differed greatly.

Over the course of two years, Mary worked with Kristin to get her Saturday early learning programs up and running, sharing ideas back and forth of successes and failures and encouraging each other when budgetary and other constraints got in the way.

Happily, Mary's new library branch soon became another official Little University location in the Denver Public Library system, giving a branded name to her already vetted Saturday programming. Even as early as the second program in Mary's Little University series, she had nearly 60 people attend a dance program in her library that accommodates little more than 85 people in total. Despite the limited space, everyone had a wonderful time!

Perhaps one of the most rewarding comments that has been made about this program was, "do you have the new Little University schedule out yet?" After less than a month, the name "Little University" was falling off the tongues of Mary's library users, and they were hungry for more.

For the purposes of this chapter, the most exciting news with which we can conclude is not the number of branch libraries in Denver now offering Little University programs, but rather that this program series model truly works in the varied communities across Denver. Successful Little University early learning programming has now unfolded and found relevance with affluent, white, college-educated households, African and Middle-Eastern immigrant and refugee populations, Latin American and Mexican

Spanish-speaking families, young "hipster" parents, and exceptionally low-income families.

It is not the program series name, the marketing tools employed, the day of the week and time, or the number of regular attendees per session that makes this program series a success, though all of these things are certainly important. Rather, it is the quite simplistic foundation on which this program is built: that of learning through play.

Starting at such an accessible place, with so few barriers to success, allows any and every curious family to attend, engage, explore, experiment, learn, and grow. As librarians, we are able to strategically and consciously form such play-based early learning programs around schedule considerations, communicate about them across varied marketing channels, and coordinate them to ensure exposure to key components of kindergarten readiness.

How we actually and literally go about coordinating this program series is where this conversation turns next.

IN SUMMARY

Each library and library system works differently. Some require extensive vetting and approval before new programs can take off, while others are more flexible. However your library system works, doing your due diligence before beginning a program like this will pay off in dividends. Here is a to-do list to help you get started:

YOUR TO-DO LIST

- Make note of your neighborhood's demographics. This can be more formally done by using census data and other information compiled from databases to which your library subscribes or more informally by simply observing who frequents the library and lives near and around it.

- Talk with families. Building a personal connection and having a conversation with families can not only provide you with the information you seek, but also build a rapport that will encourage these families to attend your programs once you get them off the ground. These conversations can be guided to help you determine programming needs, convenient days and times, and general community interest in your program.

- Brainstorm a name for the program and any branding to accompany that name. You are welcome to use "Little University," if you wish, but if you have a name that works better for your library and community, that is just as good! What is of utmost importance is that the name is one that inspires people to attend the program while also communicating some of the program's intended purpose. The branding should likewise serve this purpose: think of a logo for a clothing or electronics brand you know. Some of these brands no longer need to use the name of their company as the icon speaks for itself. If you can develop a visual like that, whether on your own or through your marketing department, you will be one step closer to making your program a household name.

- Create a list of programs that can be done with current library funding. We understand that not every library has an extensive programming budget (and some have none at all!). Chapter 4 outlines over 26 unique programming options that can be executed with little to no budget. Look there to see what programs would be of interest to your community and note them, along with any resources your library already has to make them a reality.

- Create a programming wish list. What programs would you host if your budget were unlimited? Creating a list like this helps to visualize the future possibilities of your program if (and *when*!) you secure funding for it. Take a look at Chapter 3 for over 26 exciting possibilities and note those that are of special interest to you. This is a great place to begin when inquiring about funding and what programs might be available in your community.

- Plan! Using the ideas you have developed in the previous two steps, create a schedule for your program. When will it start? How often will it take place? Will you be taking breaks? If so, when? How far ahead do you need to schedule the program for marketing purposes? How many people will you need to staff the program? Who will these people be? What materials will you need? And so on.

- Start creating marketing materials. Once you have verified interest in this program and a day and time that is convenient for your library community, the next step is to create marketing materials to sell the program. This can be as simple as a calendar template or, if you wish, you may use our sample template in the back matter. These materials do not need to be fancy, although they can be as intricate as you would like. Again, the focus is on encouraging attendance at and understanding of these programs.

- Build momentum and support among your peers. These programs cannot exist in a vacuum and cannot be realistically executed by one person. Talk to your coworkers, no matter their station or whether they work with your target age group. If everyone in your building understands the program and its purpose, it is easier to "sell" to the community. Luckily, when pitched correctly, the program more or less "sells" itself. For some ideas of elevator speeches, please see Appendix A.
- Give it a go!

THREE

Implementing the Program Series with a Budget

Both of us implemented our program series with a mixture of paid-for and free programming. Each route has distinct advantages and disadvantages, though both routes accomplish the same end goal: exposing our youngest learners to a variety of early learning opportunities for which parents do not have to pay and which they can experience alongside their little ones.

We will first discuss implementing an early learning program series with a budget and then move into ideas for early learning programs that require only a minimal, if any, budget. Keep in mind that possibilities are endless, both with and without a budget, and that these ideas and thoughts are simply what worked for our communities and what we hope might inspire you with yours.

THE CONUNDRUM OF FREE THINGS

Free things have a hidden disadvantage. Traditionally, and admittedly controversially, society does not tend to value free things. Remember how the adage "you get what you pay for" is used to refer disparagingly to the low quality of free or low-cost goods.

For the purposes of this discussion, consider how our society emphasizes the importance of certain cultural and life experiences for our children, such as trips to museums and zoos, plays and musicals, art classes and sports clubs. Even the most basic of these experiences cost money.

Examples include museums, which require membership, the zoo, which charges admission, paid-for classes like music, mommy-tot yoga, mommy-and-me art, and so on.

Needless to say, such experiences are inaccessible to many families because of that required cost.

Our early learning programming leveraged this view of paid-for experiences to the library's advantage. By bringing in early learning experiences that are traditionally paid-for, our low-income families were able to access these valued opportunities in a manner that was affordable. At the same time, these recognizable program names and familiar cultural institutions were those upon which high-income families have traditionally placed value and therefore were learning opportunities with the same perceived worth as paying for museum membership, zoo admission, class registration, and so forth.

Bringing in these paid-for programs had further benefits. One is that families knew what to do. At the zoo, for example, you see animals, make jokes, mimic the animal sounds; that sort of thing. In the art class, you paint and possibly make a mess and take home something to stick on the fridge or give to Grandma. Second, here we address both income groups: since folks attached a value to these programs greater than what they attach to storytime (unfortunately and unfairly!), this early learning program series was immediately perceived as *important*. What this allowed the library to do, then, is take all its early literacy and learning messaging up a notch. Little University programs could speak directly to learning through play and talk in a very different way than a traditional storytime format.

Not surprisingly, Little University programs revealed that both our highly educated, high-income families and our low-income, often non–English-speaking families needed the exact same learning environment, albeit for different reasons. High-income families already read at home, and they need something more than a storytime. These families are familiar with, and often choose to access, paid-for learning opportunities in the community. Seeing these available at the library feels both familiar and valuable and welcomes these families to participate. At the same time, low-income families quite often cannot participate in these paid-for learning opportunities, though they place the same value on these opportunities as other families; financial, time, and language barriers often stand between low-income families and these opportunities. Offering these programs for free at the library location these families already utilize removes these barriers to access.

In short, traditionally paid-for early learning programming opens doors: those who cannot afford it can experience it. Those who can afford it can appreciate it in a different way.

YOUR PROGRAM SERIES REFLECTS YOUR COMMUNITY

Your program presenters do not know your community and your program attendees like you do. Therefore, you should take a leading role in designing each of your programs, while they provide the niche expertise, supplies, or both. Your desire to provide early learning opportunities should not outweigh your knowledge of your community. It is critical to meet your community members where they are when developing programming.

By this, we mean it is critical to demonstrate that you as a library program designer are in touch with the community that you serve. Certainly, we would love for all our young learners to experience all the learning experiences we can possibly provide. But beginning in a place that appears out of touch with your community risks alienating your community members and unintentionally sending the message that this program series is not for them.

HOW TO APPROACH COMMUNITY PARTNERS

If you work in a larger library or library system, chances are that you already have a curated list of presenters who have passed whatever standard is required by your library system and work well with your intended audience. However, if you work at a smaller system or an independent library, you may not have a wealth of presenters from which to choose. In either case, a conversation is required to start the process of determining what kind of programming can be offered to the early learning age group.

Your pitch will sell your program. Before walking into a meeting with a potential program presenter, it is important to make sure that you have your program goals in mind. If it helps, writing them down on a piece of paper can ensure that you touch on everything that is important to you. Here are some important considerations:

- What is an early learning program?
- How does this program promote success in kindergarten and beyond?
- What kinds of programming are you hoping to offer to your families? (This is a good one to tailor to the presenter you are contacting.)

- About how many people do you expect at each program?
- What is your approximate budget per program?

Here are some questions for the presenter. The clearer everyone is leading into the program, the more successful it is likely to be.

- What is the fee for a 30-minute program?
- Does that fee include any materials the presenter will need?
- What does the presenter require from the library as far as space, set-up, and so on?
- Has the presenter worked with this age group before?
- What does the presenter know about the age group?
- What does a program for this age group look like from the presenter's perspective?

You may well come up with other questions that are specific to your location or your families in the course of preparing for this conversation and during it. These are by no means the only questions that should be asked; whatever is imperative to know on both sides in order to make a positive collaboration is critical to be considered at this point in the planning process.

It is also important to be prepared to field questions from the presenter. Remember that many of your conversations will be with community partners who have not previously considered working with this age group or have not considered working with this age group outside their location. Following are some considerations for when this is the case:

- Why have you contacted this partner?
- What program specifically can they offer your program series that is unique to their skill set and abilities?
- Why is this particular program of importance to your overall goals?
- How does this program fit into the program series as a whole?
- What might be expected after this program concludes? (For example, might you pursue additional programs with this community partner?)

DEVELOPING PROGRAMS WITH COMMUNITY PARTNERS

This section provides you with 26 program examples, including suggestions as to what community partners might provide them and how these programs directly benefit early learning. Assuming your program series meets all 52 weeks of the year and assuming you would repeat each of these programs at least one time (repetition is a key way that children learn!), this section provides you with a blueprint for a yearlong early learning program series with a budget.

This section also includes a brief note of what pitfalls you may experience when providing each program and some ideas as to how to avoid, or manage, each one. We have also included a quick note with each program should you need to do-it-yourself (DIY). We have an entire subsequent chapter dedicated to free and low-cost programming that you can DIY for your early learning series. This need-to-DIY note exists for two reasons: (1) you may find a program idea in this chapter but need or want to provide the program on your own, perhaps because you like the idea but cannot find a presenter; and (2) you may have the program scheduled with a paid-for outside presenter who needs to reschedule or cancel his or her appearance. Either way, the need-to-DIY note gives you some starting suggestions for how to pull these ideas off on your own.

Of course, these program listings are just suggestions! We have taken our most popular and successful Little University program concepts and outlined them here in a way that we hope will inspire you. We hope that these ideas, taken with your own creativity and your knowledge of your library's community, will help you create an early learning program series that is just right for where you are.

Movement Programs

Movement programs are an excellent starting point when developing an early learning program series. It is no secret that toddlers, preschoolers, and even babies enjoy moving! Movement programs build gross motor skills such as balance, coordination (often including hand-eye coordination), distinguishing left and right, and posture. Additionally, movement activities support listening, following directions, and spatial awareness (i.e., not knocking your neighbor over while you are dancing!).

Movement programs are also a great place to start when considering a budget; they often do not require supplies or use reusable supplies that the instructor already owns (e.g., soccer balls) and therefore costs only the instructors' time. In our experience, a half-hour movement program will cost $50.

When considering movement programs, your mind may wander to children with disabilities or other considerations that prohibit or impact their movement. In our experience, it has worked best to leave modifications to programs up to the child's parent or caregiver. It is difficult to assess what true limitations a child is facing, or the extent to which a parent or caregiver would like the child to "try" or to simply be exposed. Our method, which continues to work well for all involved, has been to simply welcome the child and family in the same way that each of the other children and families are welcomed and to offer to provide any help or accommodations the caregiver might like.

We have observed instances of children with movement limitations watching their parents participate in the program to parents holding children while participating as best as they can to children being allowed to try activities until they self-select to disengage. The key is to create a space that is welcoming to all and to be ready to support the child as a learner regardless of his or her ability to participate fully in the activities.

Creative Movement

Excellent for high-energy groups and a great starting point for all groups!

This program title is an affectionate way to refer to the uncoordinated and energetic gyrations that pass for dance moves as our little ones' bodies and coordination develop.

Many communities already include businesses that offer dance programs for mommies and babies, toddlers, and preschoolers. These would be excellent locations to ask to provide a program at your library, as the instructors are already familiar with dancing with this age group.

Not-for-profit agencies are also good options and may be able to provide services for your library at a reduced cost. If there is a professional dance company in your community, consider reaching out to it to see if it receives supportive arts funding from the government and if you could qualify for a program at a reduced rate.

Other community partners you might consider approaching are private dance companies. Many members of private dance companies participate as a hobby and may be interested in sharing their expertise with your families. In other cases, private dance company instructors might be willing to work with a younger age group.

Plan for families with children throughout this birth through preschool age range and prepare in advance how to welcome them to the program.

- Parents of preschool-aged children will find their little ones likely running to the front of the room to be as close as possible to the dancing action! This is entirely appropriate for this age group, as they have had more time to become confident with their bodies.

• Parents of toddlers will observe longer processing time as their little ones receive the various instructions. Encouraging them along and demonstrating the requested movements are great ways to keep them engaged and head off frustration.

• Parents of pre-walkers will have a fun but different experience with their babies. They may choose to sit to the side and hold their babies upright or help with a seated position and bounce along to the various musical rhythms. This is excellent for developing upper body strength. Tickling the babies' body parts as they are used for dancing movements is another great way to engage in the program. And jumping up and whirling the baby along with the toddlers and preschoolers simply cannot be beat! Seeing adults learning alongside children goes a long way to foster an intrinsic motivation to learn in our little ones.

If you find yourself working with a partner to develop a Creative Movement program together, the following is a helpful and successful format to follow:

1. Begin with a warm-up, and invite parents to participate right then and there! Have everyone start with seated stretches, wiggling toes, feet, fingers, hands, arms, shoulders, and heads. Stand up and reach for the sky, then the floor, then someone on their left and right (or one side, then the other, as left and right are likely to be daunting!).

2. Have your instructor introduce the concept of moving *like* something: something slow (a turtle, perhaps), something fast (a cheetah), something wiggly (a snake), something big (a bear!), something tiny (a ladybug), something delicate (a butterfly), and something huge (an elephant).

3. Then, have your instructor use their expertise to get the little ones moving. Dance instructors will be familiar with movement concepts that little ones can mimic and learn. Starting the movement portion of the program with silly animal-like movements will make your participants more comfortable trying out more-advanced concepts.

4. Encourage your instructor to use unlikely music! Perhaps a portion of a symphony would be welcome, or a quick tribute to David Bowie. Many libraries already hold a nice collection of music from around the world: a traditional French or Brazilian playground song might be fun to bop around to, or an African lullaby may be a nice, calming conclusion to a

Creative Movement program. Parents and children alike will enjoy engaging with music not traditionally used with this age group. Additionally, utilizing items from your library's collection can stimulate circulation of those items and investigation of other library offerings.

5. Freeze Dance is a particularly fun and useful activity during a Creative Movement program and a great way for you to participate along with your families. Your instructor will lead the dancing while you operate the music, inviting everyone to dance as it plays and freeze when the music pauses. Be sure to allow nice long pauses, as it will take your little ones five to seven seconds to register that it is time to hold still for a minute!

6. A wonderful way to conclude is by playing a gentle song while families snuggle their little ones close. This is especially welcome for parents of pre-walkers who may have become overstimulated by all the movement! It is even possible to talk over this sweet tune and remind parents of all their children have learned through their experiences in this program: practicing balance and coordination is no small feat for this age group!

❖ POTENTIAL PITFALLS

The potential pitfall with a Creative Movement program is the heightened energy it encourages. Be ready for a few quick breaks to calm your participants. Hopefully your instructor will come prepared with some ideas for this, too! Taking a quick minute to sit down and count backward from 10 or to switch to a very quiet song inviting slow movements are easy ways to regain control of your participants' energy. We want excitement, but we do not want anyone to get hurt!

⌘ NEED TO DIY?

There is not a toddler or preschooler alive who will notice whether you are a professional dancer or not! The basic program formula listed earlier will allow you to facilitate a great program: just find a boom box, iPhone, Bluetooth speaker, or some other way of playing music ahead of time. If you have more time to plan, check out the following chapter's suggestions for a Toddler Prom and a Disco Dance Party!

Ballet

A great program to time for the holiday season, when many cities have performances of *The Nutcracker*! A ballet program will follow much the same format as a Creative Movement program but will do even more to emphasize mind-body coordination. A ballet instructor will be able to bring even our youngest dancers into the first five ballet positions.

While learning the first five ballet positions might be the overall goal of a ballet program, experienced ballet instructors will bring a host of dancing exercises to encourage a wide variety of gross motor movements in a fun environment.

It is worth noting that a ballet program may be less interesting to parents with babies and more conducive to a group with toddlers and preschoolers. Still, parents with babies should be invited to participate in much the same way as described in the Creative Movement program section earlier.

Inviting your instructor to do a quick demonstration at the conclusion of your program is a wonderful way to help your little ones wind down and is sure to leave your families awestruck and inspired. Even watching a ballerina put on toe shoes can be an engaging experience for our little ones!

❖ POTENTIAL PITFALLS

The potential pitfall with this program is the participants' frustration. Be sure your instructor knows that we do not *actually* expect 20 toddlers to master the first five ballet positions in 30 minutes flat. Rather, we simply want to expose them to the ideas and encourage the fact that children will learn what we teach them! Some will be able to master one or two, some will get all five with gusto, and others will simply try their best or just watch. The learning is happening whether the techniques are mastered or not. Crossing a line where we are producing stress hormones instead of happy hormones will do no one any good and will certainly not encourage our families to try another Little University program. If the group appears to be generally frustrated, simply break out into a creative dance break for three minutes or so to give everyone a chance to regroup. Alternatively, cue your instructor that this would be a great time for her to perform while your families take a break to watch!

⌘ NEED TO DIY?

This one may be trickier to pull off, as it is more likely that a toddler or preschooler will notice whether you are a professional ballerina or not. Still, the nature of the program is intentional body movements taken at a slower pace. Ballet obviously provides for this, and plenty of online video tutorials will quickly orient you to the basic ballet positions. Waltzes and other slow dances provide for this too, and even if you simply lead your program attendees in mimicking each technique in a silly fashion, your attendees will accomplish what you set out to share with them that day! If you have more time to plan, pick up *Cats' Night Out* by Caroline Stutson. This picture book features cats doing a number of dance steps. You could read through it, pausing as the cats switch from one dance to the next, asking your participants to try to demonstrate what each dance might look like!

Zumba, or for This Age Group, Zumbini!

Zumbini, a registered trademark of the Zumba franchise, is a curated program that requires teachers to pass an exam and become registered with the program in order to teach it. The focus of this program is to integrate movement with song and text, bringing families together through these threads.

Typically, Zumbini is offered as a series of 6- or 12-class sessions, each building on the next so that families become more and more comfortable with the music and movement. This comfort allows families to not only be able to participate better in the program itself, but also to take those movements home with them. The repetition of these activities strengthens neural connections in babies and toddlers and promotes improvement of these skills over time. However, for the Little University format, 6 to 12 consecutive weeks of one program is not ideal. This is why it is important to coordinate ahead of time with the instructor to curate the program into one class that will be beneficial even though it will not be repeated for several weeks in a row.

Like other movement programs, Zumbini also builds coordination, strength, and balance through gross motor movements. This program combines high-intensity dance sessions to strong Latin beats with quieter, seated activities with scarves or shaker eggs. As was mentioned before, this balance helps children regulate their bodies and be better equipped to move successfully from one activity to the next.

⌘ NEED TO DIY?

While Zumba-esque classes may be intimidating to teach because of their nonstop, choreographed dance moves and cues, Zumbini does not have to follow that same format. As for the other dance programs mentioned earlier, a boom box or iPod with a speaker will do just fine to amplify sound in the programming space. There are some songs, especially for children, that guide them through movements. Find some of these either in your collection or on YouTube and follow the leader! You do not have to be the leader yourself if that makes you uncomfortable. Also, finding music with strong Latin or Afro-Cuban sounds and beats will bring the essence of Zumbini into the room while offering families and children the opportunity to move the way they are inspired to move. Linking activities like this with seated scarf songs that you already use in your storytime sessions will help put you and your participants at ease, particularly if some of them have joined your storytime sessions in the past. A warm-up and cool-down are always encouraged to help promote healthy body awareness and safety. See above for examples of these activities.

Soccer

An outstanding program for neighborhoods with families!

Yes, we are aware that our little ones cannot yet play soccer! However, there are a number of soccer-based physical literacy games that build gross motor skills while incorporating the use of a soccer ball.

Since this program is one of soccer-based games, not a soccer game itself, it requires neither a soccer field nor soccer equipment! The whole program can be accomplished with one or two portable soccer goals, a bunch of soccer balls (definitely go for one per child here!), and simple sports equipment such as pinnies and cones. And yes, it is absolutely possible to do this program inside. In fact, for safety reasons, we recommend this program be done inside!

Many communities have recreation centers and/or private organizations that provide soccer classes and camps starting at age two! These partners will be ready to work with your young age group and often come with a sense of humor that is sure to help parents feel comfortable with the chaos that will likely ensue during this program.

The soccer balls these instructors will provide for the program are designed to be used by this age group, meaning they are soft! Be sure that this is the sort of ball your instructors are planning to bring; otherwise you will need to provide helmets!

It is helpful to assist parents in orienting themselves to the goals of this program:

- Preschoolers will likely be able to engage in and follow all of the program's activities. They will likely be able to balance one foot on the soccer ball, for instance, and follow directions to learn how to dribble. This is simply because their age has allowed them enough practice with gross motor skills to try these trickier maneuvers.

- Toddlers will use this program to practice general physical literacy. They will likely not be able to follow along with the more-detailed instructions preschoolers are mastering, but will get excellent practice developing general body awareness, trying to balance on one foot and then the other and starting and stopping their bodies with the different soccer drills (games).

- Babies should stick close by parents to avoid unruly soccer balls. Parents can position babies to roll a soccer ball back and forth while older children do the more complex activities. Parents may want to hold baby's hands while she toddles along with the older children or hold the baby while helping the other children with the soccer drills. Many babies, in our experience, are perfectly happy staring wide-eyed at all the soccer excitement as parents narrate what they are seeing!

If your library location is lucky enough to be near a professional soccer team, as ours is, invite the team to send one or two players out to play along with families during this program! This will be a wonderful incentive for families to attend the program and a very exciting experience for adults and children alike. In our experience, our professional soccer team has been willing to provide library program attendees with vouchers to attend a professional soccer game at a discounted price. This would be an excellent way to continue learning as a family and promote community engagement and varied learning experiences while doing so!

Soccer programs for this age group might include the following physical literacy activities:

- Chase and Freeze Tag, played with soccer pinnies tucked in as tails that, when pulled, indicate that runner is frozen. Adding soccer balls to dribble while running will increase the difficulty of this game. Inviting parents to play along will help avoid tears and frustration when frozen.

- Red Light, Green Light, with added light colors! Instructors may add light colors to have participants do a particular task, such as balancing, dribbling, scoring a goal, this sort of thing. Our instructors, for example, have participants do a quick "Dance Party" on Purple Light!

Often enough, seeing a soccer ball that they can play with is enough to engage our young learners in a soccer program. Concluding the program with an opportunity to score a goal in a portable soccer goal and a quick group huddle (yell "Little University" on 3!) is a great way to wrap up a fun time!

❖ POTENTIAL PITFALLS

The potential pitfall with this program is an obvious one: tears. Some children will not appreciate being told what to do with their soccer ball, others will not enjoy being chased or tagged, and still others may have little use for soccer-based games when there is a soccer goal to be scored! Setting parents' expectations up to include these outcomes will help make your program a success from the start.

Reminding parents that all Little University programs are opportunities for children to practice social-emotional skills, such as sharing and trying new things, is another way to set up for success. Consider setting aside an area of the room for children who need to take a break during the program. You could even be cute and call it "the bench," and offer a cup of water to children who choose to use it. Remind parents that it is always okay to take a break if needed! And, keep yourself and your instructor in good humor throughout the program. These things will help ensure that tears do not take over the program, even if they do occur.

⌘ NEED TO DIY?

Finding 20 soft soccer balls at a moment's notice will probably be difficult. However, putting together a list of seven or eight playground games from your own childhood is well within reach! Parents will enjoy a bit of nostalgia, and those families who are unfamiliar with the games you remember will enjoy following along. In addition to Freeze Tag and Red Light, Green Light, Red Rover, Simon Says, and Duck, Duck, Goose can all be played indoors. Have the children pair up with their parents for a few rounds of Hand Clap rhythms. You can lead, or they can create their own. Then organize everyone for Seven Up for a quiet finish. If you have more time to plan, make a Hopscotch challenge out of masking tape on your floor, and/or put together a version of the Floor Is Lava as an obstacle course. Granted, there are no soccer balls to entice, but these games still accomplish the goals of practicing balance and building overall physical literacy.

Sing- and Dance-Along Programs

A better movement program for groups with lots of pre-walkers! Singing and dancing together is a time-tested way to have a wonderful time. Parents will likely be more comfortable in this setting, as they can do the singing while the little ones take care of the dancing. Look for community partners that offer kid-friendly concerts. Our favorite is a one-man-band performer who plays the guitar while singing and playing a harmonica here and there; his getup alone is exciting for our young children to see!

With this particular program, room setup is important. Position your parents in a large circle and invite children to sit with their grown-ups in a lap-sit sort of way. Invite your musician to be in the center of the circle, moving around throughout his song lineup. As children become more comfortable and get excited, encourage them to hop up and dance along in the center of the circle along with the performer. It may help to ensure that one or two songs on the list have structured dance movements. "The Wheels on the Bus" and "Old MacDonald" are excellent and familiar songs with movement suggestions built right in. You might also try the "Hokey Pokey" and "Shake Your Sillies Out."

A second approach to this program idea is to locate a performer who provides cultural musical experiences. We enjoy a performer who presents music from around the world, played and sung on a variety of interesting instruments. Playing songs from other cultures is both exciting and educational, stretching everyone's brains with different rhythms and languages. Even more wonderful is if your performer knows the traditional dances that accompany the songs. This version of the program is a bit more in-depth, but it is a lovely way to introduce families to music they might not otherwise encounter and still accomplish the goal of gross motor movement.

❖ POTENTIAL PITFALLS

A potential pitfall of this program is if no one is singing! This might especially be the case if the songs are from other cultures and are therefore unfamiliar to your families. This is where you come in, as someone perfectly positioned to lead by example. Sit with your families in the circle and try to sing along with your performer. If this is out of reach, clapping, patting your knees, and snapping your fingers are all great ways to participate along with the music. And, of course, this program is intended to be a movement program, so having the children participating in the music with their bodies is still the ultimate goal whether parents are helping boost the volume or not! If you are concerned about the potential lack of participation from your audience, ask the presenter ahead of time if he or she would be comfortable providing a song sheet with lyrics that you could copy and provide for parents who prefer to know all of the words before jumping in to singing. If you have an overhead projector screen, this is another way to incorporate that text if necessary.

⌘ NEED TO DIY?

You may be an accomplished guitarist or ukulele player with a repertoire of children's songs under your belt; but then again, you may not be. We suggest you make a quick mental list of all the songs you are familiar with presenting to children, perhaps from previous storytime experiences. Almost every children's song that comes to mind has some opportunity for movement. About 10 or so of these songs will be plenty for your last-minute Sing- and Dance-Along programs. Gather your parents in the aforementioned circle and launch into your first tune. "If You're Happy and You Know It" is always a winning place to start. Clap your hands, stomp your feet, and incorporate any other movements that come to you to make these songs sound loud and proud! Your DIY version of this program may not have the thrill of a one-man-band, but you will still accomplish the singing and, most importantly, the gross motor movements of dancing as the little ones get involved in the music. And, if singing is absolutely not in your skill set, grab some CDs from your library's collection and let them do the work! If you have chosen this program because you have more pre-walkers than other ages, concluding with a snuggly round of "Twinkle, Twinkle Little Star" is an excellent way to bring the energy back to ground level.

Tumbling

Try it at your own risk! Now this is an incredibly fun, and unlikely, early learning program. As we all probably agree, little ones are built like noodles; their flexibility never ceases to amaze. Tumbling is a great way to channel that flexibility into gross motor movements that promote strength and coordination.

Your local recreation center likely has a parent-tot tumbling class already, which may build into toddler and preschool gymnastics classes. Many communities also have private gymnasiums that offer such classes for the birth through preschool age group. Ask about observing one or two of these classes to see what they are like and to reassure yourself that they do not end in broken bones or other injuries!

Most tumbling classes are set up as obstacle courses. Mirroring the afore-mentioned soccer program, the classes involve more gross motor games and less actual tumbling. The tumbling instructor you invite will bring a carload of gym mats, hula hoops, and other obstacle course props for your program, so be sure to have plenty of open space set aside for this one!

As always, orienting parents to the goals of the program will help ensure success. Your tumbling instructor should help you with this introduction to ensure that safety is the top consideration. The instructor will likely demonstrate how parents with babies can guide them through the various exercises and then show how toddlers and preschoolers will be participating on their own, most likely.

A typical tumbling program will begin with a series of group warmups followed by somewhat tricky exercises like Jumping Jacks. Then, parti-cipants will be invited to try the various stations set up throughout the space. They will likely simply repeat these stations as desired, usually going through in a lineup and waiting for each turn. After three to four rotations, most will have mastered almost all of the tasks. Your instructor will then bring everyone back together for a group wrap-up.

❖ POTENTIAL PITFALLS

The glaring potential pitfall with this program is the likelihood for injury. Thus, the somewhat humorous announcement to "try it at your own risk!" Experienced instructors, however, are truly masters at preventing injury. Be sure whomever you bring in to facilitate your program has been appropriately trained, and be sure your parents know that if anything looks like too much for them that it is ok to just skip it! The second pitfall is much more likely than injury: that your little ones will have no use for going in order through the sta-tions or waiting their turn for each station. This will be especially true after round one, at which point all of the children will have found a favorite and want to simply repeat that one activity for the remaining 20 minutes of the program. Remind your families that waiting and taking turns is part of life and that the part of the program that promotes that is just as beneficial to their little ones as the tumbling parts of the program. Invite parents whose children are truly not having it to either take a break, or to stay in line, walk past the undesirable sta-tions in their place in line, and then only participate in the station of interest.

⌘ **NEED TO DIY?**

Unless you are a certified tumbling instructor, we recommend skipping that part of this program. Still, there are a number of indoor games you can play that will get the little ones moving! Start by introducing the concept of a race: that is, making it from one side of your space to the other. Try one round walking in slow motion to give everyone time to orient themselves, then maybe a quick sprint. From there, expand into hopping races, skipping races, and sideways walking races. Backward walking races are especially tricky, but try one if your group is still willing to move slowly. Next, do a Crab-Walk Race, a Bear-Walk Race, a Bunny-Hop Race, or a Frog-Hop Race. Even babies can get into the game if parents jump in there with them! Go ahead and try those Jumping Jacks. Teach them one step at a time, and work your way up to moving faster and faster. These are very difficult for this age group to perform but are incredibly beneficial for gross motor development. Again, even your babies can get into it with parents bringing their arms overhead and then back down by their sides. You can teach Push Ups the exact same way! Invite your group to try a round of Pushover Parent, where the little ones try to knock their parents over. Engaged parents will make this especially fun, and perhaps you have grandparents with you that day who are willing to get in on the action! If you are comfortable doing so, you might invite the children to play a quick round of Pushover Librarian, too! Tickle Tag is a great way to wrap up this lively program, and again, engaged parents will make this a wonderful activity. Babies will enjoy being tickled, too! If you have more time to prepare, blow up some balloons and play Balloon Ball, with the goal being to keep the balloons from touching the ground. Start with only two or three, then gradually add more until you are up to almost one balloon per participant! Pick up several containers of bubble mix and have your parents help you blow bubbles for the children to pop or for the babies to reach for! An entire bubble program is also listed in the following chapter. And going along with this theme, lay down several sheets of bubble wrap on your floor and invite your children to help hop all over the wrap until all the bubbles are popped.

STEM Programs

STEM (science, technology, engineering, and math) programs are some of the most important and often underrepresented programs for this age group. This is due to a variety of factors, the primary one being that those facilitating programs are usually more comfortable teaching art and movement-based programs than those in the STEM realm. Math and science can be intimidating to people who received liberal arts degrees in college and may only have taken the basic math and science courses to graduate.

However, it is important for caregivers and librarians alike to recognize the myriad times that STEM reaches into everyday life in fun and creative ways. Not only does this make adults more comfortable, but it also introduces young children to these concepts at a young age, thus improving their overall understanding of the world around them.

It is also important to note that the children in your programs will not be expected to solve differential equations by the end of a math-themed session (and neither will you!) STEM concepts at this age are much more tactile and approachable, and there are many ways to make them fun, as you will see in the programs outlined here.

Nature and Science Museum Programs

Not all science programs have to be experiments, but some can be!

A nature and science museum is an excellent learning space, but one that parents of young children may not feel comfortable bringing young children to. Inviting museum educators to your early learning program series is an excellent way to introduce natural history and science, including outer space, to a very young audience!

Many museums already have an educator or docent on staff, who is equipped to provide educational experiences for school groups or even younger children. Some museums may even have learning spaces set up specifically for younger children. Contacting museums in your community and inquiring about these opportunities is the first place to begin.

From there, the key is determining what exhibits and artifacts travel easily enough to bring to your library program. Many museums have replicas of fossils, for example, that travel easily. Other options might include artifacts set aside specifically for touching and handling. Still other options may not be artifacts at all, but instead might be science experiments that can be demonstrated and replicated.

Overall, the focus of a nature and science museum program should be STEM concepts: vocabulary around describing our observations in detail, exploration of different materials, narrative discussion around experiments, this sort of thing. A program like this should begin by introducing one or two simple concepts or terms, providing an activity or experiment first demonstrated, then replicated by each child and their caregiver, and then a concluding discussion. A take-home component is always an excellent addition if available!

❖ **POTENTIAL PITFALLS**

Potential pitfalls here center on artifacts getting damaged or experiments going wrong. The opportunity for messiness here is high if experiments are being conducted. Museum educators should anticipate the possibility of damaged artifacts and avoid bringing, for example, a newly discovered dinosaur bone. Items that can be replaced are clearly ideal. Using this as a learning opportunity is advised; prepare children to touch with gentle hands, using one or two fingers only. Similarly, prepare children to conduct experiments using slow hands, and help parents prepare for spills and the like by giving them specific portions of the experiment to conduct for their children. Lastly, should experiments not work as planned, simply use this as a teaching moment, and discuss together as a group what *did* happen and how you reacted to what happened (i.e., with surprise, with frustration, with pleasure, etc.).

⌘ **NEED TO DIY?**

You can! There are a number of science experiments using simple kitchen products, and instructions are available online. Even mixing up your own bubble mix will suffice (fashion bubble wands out of pipe cleaners if you have them!) Play-Doh can be made from items on a grocery store shelf and will give you much to discuss in terms of how each ingredient feels compared to how the final product feels. (Tip: Get some Ziploc bags for everyone to take their Play-Doh home in, and skip the food coloring to avoid unnecessary dying of hands!)

Plant Programs

The learning just goes on and on! Most communities have a botanical garden, community garden space, or even a gardening store. Connecting with these organizations/businesses is a great way to bring a gardening program to your series. These are particularly timely in the spring and around Earth Day. Adventurous program providers might also seek out gardening programs that focus on cold weather plants specifically.

Plant programs can go in one of several directions, but we hope your programs move past the radish-in-the-cup-of-soil model. Engaging children with their natural environments is the key here, but again, there are many ways to do this. Our advice on plant programs focuses on three varieties:

1. A gardening program, during which children will first be introduced to different types of plants: flowers, vegetables, trees, and so forth. Many organizations are able to bring examples of these different plants that children can then touch, observe, smell, and perhaps even taste! This program will then move into a planting project, but preferably one using starter plants as opposed to seeds. This will increase the likelihood of success once the plants are taken home. An ideal gardening program might also include exhibiting the seeds that then grow into the plants being studied. Overall, this program invites lots of tactile experiences and encourages expanding vocabulary.

2. A terrarium program, which focuses more on soil than on plants. Families would be provided with jars in which to make a terrarium to take home and then introduced to the layers of soil that contribute to a healthy plant. Heads up! One layer is generally charcoal, which is messy to touch but also a surprising opportunity to draw or write during this program! As each type of soil is introduced, children should scoop a handful or cupful into their terrarium. The finishing touch will of course be a small plant and then a quick primer on how to effectively water it. Ideal terrarium programs might include plastic bugs to add to the jars. Like the gardening program, this program provides plenty of tactile experiences and a great chance to learn new vocabulary words. A talented program facilitator can usually stump parents on different properties of soil!

3. An eating program, which focuses on the products of plants: where our food comes from. A fantastic option for this sort of plant program is a salsa-making class. Tomato plants, jalapeno plants, onions, garlic, and cilantro all travel quite easily. Even lemon or lime trees are possible to transport. An educator would bring one of each of these plants to show and discuss and then use the fruits of the plant to lead the families through making salsa. (For large groups, have your instructor chop everything up ahead of time, and give each family a bowl to scoop ingredients into and mix. Smaller groups would allow each family to chop ingredients on their own and then mix. Either way, go easy on the hot pepper!) Add some chips, and this is always a winner. Ideal programs might include a small cilantro plant for each family to take home.

❖ POTENTIAL PITFALLS

Potential pitfalls here are relatively few. We suggest gathering an armload of old newspapers ahead of time to cut down on messiness and make cleanup a breeze. If educators are bringing plants for participants to take home, encourage them to bring all the same type of plant to eliminate children having to choose which plant they would like. Lastly, remind parents at the outset that children should wash hands after handling plants or dirt to avoid contaminating eyes, noses, or mouths with substances that should not be introduced to those parts of our bodies.

⌘ NEED TO DIY?

If you have time to prepare to do this program on your own, you will be just fine. We recommend going to your nearest gardening center and buying a huge bag of potting soil. Grab a flat of plants that look relatively healthy (mint and other herbs are particularly hardy and fragrant) and if you have the budget for it, enough small terra cotta pots for your group. (This sounds expensive, but generally should cost about $3–5 per participant, including the plant, pot, and soil. Skip the little tray that sits underneath the pot to save money.) Short on either time or funding? Find yourself some egg cartons and dirt, and then grab a couple of packs of radish or green bean seeds. (To compare, this will cost about $3–5 for your entire group!) Read a picture book like *Growing Vegetable Soup* (Lois Ehlert) to your group, and then have everyone help fill each section of the egg carton with soil and two or three seeds. Keep these in your library for about 10 days: long enough for them to sprout. You'll want them on the windowsill of your office, and you'll obviously want to water them a few times! Then, cut the egg cartons into individual sections and hand the starter plants out to your group at your next early learning program! Alternately, plant the starters into your library landscaping or a nearby community garden with a sign indicating they were cultivated by your early learning program!

Live Animals

A classic that simply cannot be beat! Whenever families see the words "zoo" or "live animals" on a program announcement, you can be sure that you will have excellent turnout for that program. There is something about live animals that draws people in, especially when it is possible to get up close and even touch them! The zoo itself is great, but as mentioned earlier, it usually requires some sort of fee to enter and there are few opportunities to get to study animals up close and personal without a dividing barrier.

Zoos are often nonprofit and receive funding from the city or other agencies. This fact can mean that businesses like libraries can sometimes receive scholarships to be able to host programs at their locations for a smaller fee. Inquire about this possibility or if there might be another mutually beneficial way for you to work together.

Zoos, however, are not the only places that offer programs with animals. In our experience, there are several organizations around the city that provide excellent animal-based programs that sometimes are themed, whether to Harry Potter or other pop-culture references or simply to whatever animal type is being presented. Depending on your audience and what you hope to accomplish with each program, you will be able to determine which organization makes sense to you at any given time.

Organizations will tend to show one animal at a time. Help your participants be successful by taking the transitions as an opportunity to get little ones' wiggles out. The children will need to sit relatively still and be relatively quiet to avoid spooking animals, so jumping up for a song and dance will help them fulfill the more tedious requirements of the program. Educators facilitating the program might get into the idea and join along themselves!

❖ POTENTIAL PITFALLS

One potential pitfall is that some organizations do not know what animals will be brought in advance of the program for various reasons. For those with anxieties about animals or with a desire to know what the program will entail ahead of time, this can be very off-putting. One recommendation to these families is to remind them that all animals share space on the Earth, and if any of them make the child or caregiver uncomfortable, they always have the right not to touch that animal if it is offered or to step outside the room briefly. However, facing fears (especially if the fear is primarily that of the caregiver) can help the child to experience the world with as little bias as possible.

⌘ NEED TO DIY?

This one will obviously be much harder to accomplish because it is rare that the library will have a gecko or hissing cockroach or butterfly on hand to show children and families. However, the library is filled with nonfiction texts about different animals, and this could be a perfect time to introduce families to the wonder that is found in these nonfiction texts. Listening to animal sounds on a speaker, watching videos of animals using library DVDs, and creating animal footprints using stamps or clay are excellent alternatives that still provide an important learning opportunity for children and their caregivers.

Entertainment

There is a place for this too! Plenty of magic is science! Entertainment programs are an excellent way to kick off your early learning program series, or to accommodate dates you may have larger groups of participants than normal (i.e., holiday weekends with extended family members in town or during your summer reading months).

Seek out local performers who provide entertainment programs for young children. Asking your nearby preschools if they have worked with anyone like this is a great place to start, or search for performers who provide birthday party entertainment. From here, work in partnership with the entertainer to put together a half-hour presentation that will both entertain and educate your group.

Remember, any experience can be a learning experience if framed as such! Three to five magic tricks with a how-to following them will be enough to fill your program time. Or, bring in a balloon twister who teaches parents how to twist balloons into simple animals, and then parents can make a creation for their children. An ideal program would conclude with a magic trick the kids can attempt themselves. Poking a needle through a balloon is a great option for this, or balancing a peacock feather upright in their hand.

Other entertainment options work well here too! Acrobats, or entertainers who practice physical theater, can provide discussion about gravity. So can jugglers! Face painters might be hired in conjunction with an animal-oriented program. Essentially, any performer who can entertain at a children's birthday party can also educate your group, so long as you and your performer frame the learning as such.

❖ POTENTIAL PITFALLS

Potential pitfalls here include the fear factor. Clowns tend to scare children (and many adults!) rather than entertain them, so steer clear of this sort of program provider. Similarly, balloons popping can be unnecessarily startling, so invite children anxious about this to wait outside the room for their balloon creation to be completed, and then pick it up. Most entertainment programs are the sit-and-watch type, so overall pitfalls here are relatively few.

⌘ NEED TO DIY?

We assume you are not secretly a unicyclist or stilt walker, though if you are you will have the DIY program of this type well in hand! Rather than scrambling to perform for your group, try putting together four to six party activities and have a big Un-Birthday Party for everyone! Create an obstacle course with hula hoops and pool noodles, have an egg and spoon race (with hardboiled eggs or plastic Easter eggs!), and set up a photo booth filled with weird disguises (boas, old sunglasses, big hats, fake mustaches, etc.) for parents to snap pictures of their children (and themselves!) in. Invite everyone to make an easy craft by taping a paper plate onto a paint stirring stick to form a bat, and then blowing up a balloon to play balloon-baseball with. Bring your group together with a less stressful version of musical chairs: Pass the Bag. (If you haven't played it, simply fill a grocery sack with clothing items and pass from person to person in a circle as you play music. When the music stops, whoever has the bag must reach inside without looking and put on whatever article of clothing they come out with first! This will have the little ones cackling as they watch their dads or grandparents try to fit into a kid-sized T-shirt or tennis shoe!) Last but not least, finish your event with a balance beam made out of masking tape on your floor, and invite each child from your group to try walking heel-toe, tip-toe, and so on from one end to the other—with the ending point being your spot to wish them farewell as they leave for the day! This DIY version will not incorporate as much STEM as the hired performer entertainment program, but it will still entertain your group and build more social-emotional skills than a sit-and-watch program might.

Building

Here is where the engineering comes into play-based learning! Building with children this age might invoke immediate fears of smashed fingers, but there are a number of ways to approach building programs that are conducive to this age group! Plus, even programs that do involve actual tools are possible with caregivers right there to help with the tough parts.

There are a number of places to look for a building program presenter.

- You might try your local hardware store to see if there is a wood-worker in your community who might like to cut pieces to a project that families could then assemble, such as wooden pieces to a bird-house or a cornhole game.
- You might already have a craft shop in your community that special-izes in handiwork programs that could be simplified for this age group.
- You may be near one or more big-box stores that could supply materi-als and design advice for your program participants to complete a project under your own instruction.

Successful building programs do tend to involve tools and other "actual" building supplies, such as nails or hot glue guns. Therefore, caregiver involvement is key. Your presenter will begin with safety instructions and hopefully provide safety glasses, aprons, and gloves for each child to bor-row for the duration of the program. Your presenter will then introduce the project that will be made, with each child creating their own version of the project. Birdhouses are a great starting spot, since their assembly is straightforward and wood glue can stand in for hammers and nails. Toy cars are simple to build, and an open time to tinker with various materials is always an option. Your presenter should be prepared to provide basic instruction and to step in to assemble and assist should any caregiver be uncertain as to how to proceed. One building project will likely take your entire program time slot and may require additional time to wrap up. We encourage you to conclude with decorating whatever project has been built, a task all children can help with whether they are babies finger paint-ing or preschoolers providing exact detailed trim.

❖ POTENTIAL PITFALLS

The top potential pitfall here is the obvious one: tools can injure as easily as they can build. Orienting caregivers to the fact that using tools is the point of this program, rather than an incidental addition, is key. Giving children an opportunity to practice self-control will also give them an opportunity to try a new skill. However, not all parents will be ready for comfortable with this con-cept, and that is okay too. Rather than pushing parents out of their comfort zones, provide some instruction as to how they can do the heavy lifting while their child is still involved. The easiest option here is to have the parents do the dangerous steps while the child passes them the next material needed. And, if you've allowed time for decorating, the program will finish with each child having the chance to directly interact with their project, if not with the actual tools.

⌘ NEED TO DIY?

There are a couple of ways to approach this. We doubt you'd have access to the machinery necessary to prepare multiple birdhouse kits in advance, nor are you likely to have 20 pairs of child-sized safety glasses and children's hammers lying around. You could, however, provide the materials to make junk robots. These can be as simple or as involved as you would like. Wood glue and or hot glue (this being the caregiver's job!) will hold the robot together, as will electrical tape and duct tape. Milk cartons, tin cans, and other materials from the recycling bin will make up the robots' bodies, and all sort of accoutrements can be added on as eyes, ears, antennae, and buttons. Other DIY building projects might include milk carton birdhouses or insect hotels. For these, simply add cardboard bases and a whole bunch of popsicle sticks to the mix. If you are presenting on your own, inviting your families to take time to figure out *how* to build a project will go a long way toward fulfilling the engineering component of STEM programming!

Art Programs

Art, particularly for this age group, is a relative concept. No person, not Monet or Picasso or Kahlo, was a proficient artist at age three. So throw all of those preconceived ideas out of the window! Art at this age can be a form of expression, but it is also a critical component to encouraging the skills necessary for writing. It is important to remind parents throughout the program that, no matter what is being done, it is most important to focus on the *process* instead of the *product*. Modeling language and behavior that support this will help parents get the right idea: "You just drew a circle with red paint!" is much more positive a phrase to use than "You drew a line. Now, draw another one like this and you get a T! We can keep going and write your name." Though parents may dream of the day when their child can write on their own, programs for this age group should be more focused on encouraging discovery rather than dictating forward momentum.

Touch, manipulation of objects, color, and more are all part of art. Music and theater have a place here, too! As these programs are disappearing from schools, building a strong foundation and love for them from an early age can encourage continued exploration and interest into childhood and adolescence.

Visual Arts

Don't forget to include your art museums! Art programs are always a welcome addition to an early learning program series. Caregivers find art projects easily accessible and appreciate that the mess and cleanup is occurring somewhere other than their kitchen table!

This being said, it is imperative to emphasize that art programs are about process over product, as mentioned earlier. To do this inherently, focus on art programs that center on exploration of materials rather than a prescriptive project. Involving art museum educators as program presenters is a great way to do just that!

Art museum educators are usually experienced in providing artwork play spaces for little ones. This allows children to experiment with art materials as well as everyday objects. Tempera paint (nontoxic and washable) and large sheets of thick white paper provide the backdrop for this program. Presenters can almost always provide smocks or large T-shirts for children to wear while working. Children can explore the paint on paper with their fingers first. Then, presenters can provide children with a variety of objects to use to paint with: Duplos, celery sticks or cut potatoes, cotton balls and Q-tips, and sticks are some that we have seen used with success. Children will effectively stamp or roll with these objects, creating patterns on their paper. Once they have had the opportunity to explore in this fashion, a new sheet of paper might be distributed, and paint brushes might be introduced at this time. Overall, the goal of this program is practicing fine motor skills.

Opportunities for cultural exploration abound! Art museum educators might consider bringing artifacts or replicas of artifacts that children can touch and explore before beginning their own artwork. Alternately, educators might bring hard copies of different painting to pass around to participants and ask children and caregivers to help describe each. This will set the stage for a variety of artistic styles to be welcome at your program, including those of babies, toddlers, and preschoolers!

❖ POTENTIAL PITFALLS

Potential pitfalls here are two: the first is the potential for mess. Washable paint is a must as it is guaranteed to be on hands, arms, and even faces by the end of this program. You might suggest to parents ahead of time that children should wear old clothes for this program, even if smocks are to be provided. You should also cover your floor or table with newspapers or plastic tablecloths to prevent damage to your library's property. The second pitfall is caregivers insisting on valuing product over process. In this case, you might offer that family two sheets of white paper: one on which the child can explore and the other on which he can create a piece of art for the refrigerator.

⌘ NEED TO DIY?

You'll want to grab washable tempera paint and thick white paper, which are imperative. If you are able to get paintbrushes, even better. Consider that with the paint, you only need red, yellow, and blue. Grab about 20 different objects that you don't mind getting paint on, or that you don't mind washing paint off. Even office supplies (larger than choking hazard size!) will work here. Your DIY version of this program might begin by mixing your three primary colors to create orange, green, and purple. Have your paints separated by color in bowls of some sort (cups are a bit narrow for children this age to work with). Invite your families to start by exploring with one or two fingers on paper to create a finger painting. Then, introduce the found objects to the group and invite them to explore painting with those objects. If you've managed to get paintbrushes, take a minute to clear up the found objects and set the wet papers aside before introducing the paintbrushes with a clean sheet of white paper. Wrap up your program with this time of creating one painting with a paintbrush.

Kitchy and Cutesy Projects

There is a place for these, and they really do make great gifts! Now is when we can discuss a product that is as important as the process of making it! We suggest timing these programs around holiday weekends, where families might be interested in creating handmade gifts with their little ones or extended family members might be in town to join the program and create a piece of memorabilia with grandchildren, nieces, or nephews.

These programs are excellent ways to include local businesses in your area, in your early learning program series. Reach out to mommy-and-me painting studios or ceramics studios that offer DIY programming. Studio owners can often find a way to transport enough materials to your location to provide their usual projects at your site. In the case of ceramics, this may involve taking projects back to the studio to fire before returning the finished product back to the library for pick up, which could result in a more costly program given the amount of time the provider is investing in it.

In the case of these programs, we are thinking beyond coiled clay pots and hand-printed pottery tiles. Popular gift-making programs we have facilitated with success have involved thumbprint painting on ceramic coffee mugs, fused glass necklace charms, and canvas paintings of handprints and footprints. Your program presenter should take the lead on determining what would work best for your group in your location.

❖ POTENTIAL PITFALLS

The top potential pitfall of this program is the project not working out as expected. A sense of humor will go a long way in this instance. Also, preparing your presenter ahead of time for this possibility will help immensely; let them know that the ultimate goal is still providing an opportunity to practice fine motor skills, and assure them they will be compensated whether the projects turn out or not. After this, you might plan to allow parents and children extra time for this program. You might also consider asking the presenter to plan for a practice round before the final product is made. Lastly, you might help particularly stressed parents (those determined to make a well-turned-out present, for example) find a way to construct the project they want for their child, and then allow the child to fill in details. This, obviously, is not the ideal experience for the early learner but can make the difference between a family returning for another program in the series, or never returning at all.

⌘ NEED TO DIY?

If you have time to plan ahead, you can pick up a marble artwork painting kit. Don't worry, no marbles are involved! This is a simple and mesmerizing process of creating a marbled appearance on paper. Grab a packet of blank greeting cards, and allow your families to make sets of cards to take home. You will begin your program by demonstrating the process needed to create this type of art and then have multiple stations set up for families to take turns doing their printing. One kit will easily accommodate 20 families making four to five cards each. You will spend your time during the program changing out the water needed to create the designs. Since these cards take little time to dry, they will be ready to go home almost as soon as your families gather their things to leave! If you are unable to get this kit ahead of time, take a look at the DIY painting suggestion above as a last-minute plan for providing this program on your own.

Musical Instruments

Kids can play these! And make these! Just like with visual arts, exploration of music at this age is more about the process than about the product. Again, no child will be expected to compose a symphony by the program's end. However, children will be expected to try as many instruments as they can depending on the nature of the program.

Local music programs, including not-for-profit and folk centers, will, in our experience, be more than happy to bring their program to your library to encourage and facilitate a love of music. One successful program we have experienced is the Instrument Petting Zoo, where an organization brings in a variety of instruments for children to play that can be banged around, stepped on, and more as children explore them. Programs like this expose children to instruments that they may not have the opportunity to touch or manipulate otherwise because they are expensive or fragile.

❖ POTENTIAL PITFALLS

A potential pitfall of this program is the noise. In a separate room where the door can be closed or which is sufficiently far from others in the library who are attempting to do quiet study and focus, this program works just fine. It also provides people the opportunity to step out as they need to if they get overwhelmed or need a break. In a smaller building, however, or one without a separate space for these types of programs, this can become tricky. The more children there are, the more noise there will inevitably be. While the program will only last about 30 minutes, it may adversely affect the sanity of your staff members and other library users if they cannot escape the noise level. Another note of confusion that we have faced with our customers is the fact that, while the word "zoo" is used in the title, there will actually be no animals present. This may require some clarification for families wishing to attend the program if it is unclear from the title alone.

⌘ **NEED TO DIY?**

While you may not have 30 ukuleles laying around your library, chances are that you have access to things like shaker eggs, rhythm sticks, and/or bells. If this is the case, use these! While they may not be as exciting as the drums or tambourines that your program provider might have brought, they still make rhythm and sound. In a pinch, you can have these available to your families and play a variety of music in the background while exploring how each sound fits with the music. Even better is to guide your families through these sounds with each instrument, experimenting together with fast and slow, loud and soft, and so on.

Singing

There's nothing like bonding through music—with your own child and with your community members! Now this is a fun program and another easily accessible program from your families' point of view! Singing together can take a variety of forms, but in this case, we are referring to a program where caregivers and children are invited to sit together and sing their hearts out for a half an hour.

Your program presenter should be lively and ideally able to play one or more instruments. Your local music school would be a great place to start searching for a program presenter. The presenter should come with his or her instrument(s) and song sheets printed with lyrics for all participants. Presenters might consider including one or more songs in other languages; nothing too complex though, as you want caregivers to feel comfortable joining in with the singing. Think "Frère Jacques."

Families should be oriented to the benefits of singing together at the start of this program. Not only does singing together invite special bonding time with little ones, but it also slows words down into separate syllables to prepare children to sound out words successfully when reading.

An ideal song lineup will begin with very familiar songs that incorporate simple finger plays or silly sounds, such as "The Wheels on the Bus" and "Old MacDonald." Beginning with easy, familiar songs will encourage your participants to jump right in to the singing. The middle section of your program should include louder songs with longer, more complex verses, and opportunities for gross movement for the little ones. Such songs might include "The Silly Dance Contest" and lively folk music. This will be the time where caregivers can stretch their comfort zones by singing songs unfamiliar to them. A good program presenter will have a number of ways to be sure participants are doing this in a way that feels safe and fun. We suggest ensuring that your program conclude with quiet, relaxing songs that invite sitting, hugging, and snuggling. Perhaps even consider turning out the lights for the conclusion of your singing program to invite calm and peace back into your space. Your presenter might begin this section by singing a soft song *to* your group, as children and caregivers settle back down together. Then the group might conclude with "Twinkle, Twinkle Little Star" and other lullabies. Caregivers should mark success by having the opportunity to practice familiar songs in a group setting and the opportunity to learn one or two new songs to sing at home with their children.

❖ POTENTIAL PITFALLS

Potential pitfalls for this program are very few! The primary pitfall to anticipate is lack of participation. A confident program presenter will be able to roll with few to no caregivers singing along and still provide a quality experience for the children. Your own participation in the singing, though, will help prevent this situation from occurring. Ensuring all caregivers have song sheets to inform them of lyrics will also go a long way toward ensuring participation.

⌘ NEED TO DIY?

We are sure you know enough simple songs to provide a program like this on your own, even without accompanying yourself with a musical instrument. Should this not be a situation you are confident about, there are other options! Consider pulling CDs from your library's collection and using those as the basis for a sing-along. If you have musical instruments (such as shakers or rhythm sticks), get those out to add to the excitement. Using the formula of lap-sit, then gross movement, and then quiet snuggling will ensure a fun and informative program for your families whether you are directing the singing or a recorded voice is leading the way.

Theater

Get your local thespians involved! Now is the time to involve community members with a flair for the dramatic! Programs based on books may seem rudimentary in an early learning program series; however, asking a local actor to provide a program centered on a book will ensure that a book-based program goes beyond the traditional storytime!

Look for children's theater actors to present this program. Work with your presenter to select a book that is lively and provides ample opportunity for fun engagement. The more dramatic, the better! *Again!* by Emily Gravett is a great place to start.

Have your presenter begin the program by introducing the book by reading it dramatically to the group. Acting out specific characters while reading, doing different voices, and alternating volumes will both play to your presenter's talents and engage your families. Then, your presenter should ask your group to help them act out the story. Begin this segment with simple preparatory exercises such as stretching bodies and practicing different voice types (a squeaky voice, a loud voice, a grumpy voice, and a tired voice are examples of this). When the presenter feels the group is ready—warming up to this point is always fun!—he or she will bring the book back out. The presenter will then reread the story, but with the children and caregivers acting along. So for example, the presenter will read a sentence, demonstrate how the character talks and acts, and then ask each the group to do this along with him or her. A steady pace that builds rapidly toward the conclusion of the book will make this a lively success. Presenters might also bring along props to further enliven the group, where children can act out while dressed as the main book character (a dragon, for instance!) Your program will conclude with the participants clapping for the story they have all helped bring to life.

❖ POTENTIAL PITFALLS

As with a singing program, potential pitfalls here are few. Children love to dress up and playact, or role-play. Caregiver involvement can be in-depth; for example, caregivers might be asked to act out the adult roles in the story while children act out the child or animal roles. But, caregiver involvement can be relatively limited, and still the program can be successful. If caregivers are reluctant to participate, your presenter should still be able to effectively lead the group of children through actions and voices while caregivers simply watch or take pictures.

⌘ **NEED TO DIY?**

You can! Anyone with experience providing storytimes likely has a flair for engaging reading. While you may not be as comfortable as a professional performer acting out a story on your own, you certainly can choose lively books to engage your families. If providing this program on your own, we recommend choosing three different books that invite gross movement. *We're Going on a Bear Hunt* is an obvious choice here, but also consider books by Jan Thomas, which naturally invite gross motor movements. We recommend starting with an accessible book, such as *From Head to Toe* by Eric Carle. Then move into a book that will be more engaging and less familiar, like one of your Jan Thomas selections. Conclude with a book that invites both sitting and participation, such as *Press Here* by Hervé Tullet. This particular selection has the added bonus of concluding your program with a huge round of applause!

Art Installations

Even children this young can participate in a group art project! An amazing way to build community with your group is to engage together in a group art project. This project might become an installation in your library building, a temporary display in your children's section, or simply a part of your programming space. You might even create an installation that lives outside your library building, like a community garden or an outdoor art walk.

The first step to setting up a program of this type likely goes without saying: getting permission to add an installation to your library space. From this point, you will want to hire a program presenter from your community whose expertise and experience match the sort of installation you would like to create. The simplest sort of installation would be tiled artwork, so we will use this as our example.

Your presenter should be prepared to prep amply in advance and to stay after the program time has ended to install the artwork appropriately. Because of this added commitment, this program is likely to cost more than most. Children this young will likely find it too tedious to work together as a group on one project. Rather, each family will need to be able to create a single piece of the installation on their own. In the case of the tiled artwork, the presenter should begin by presenting the overall concept, hopefully with visual aids. The presenter might have tied the concept to a familiar storybook, such as one by Dr. Seuss or Eric Carle. A quick reading of the story will help orient your families to the concept of what you all are creating together. Then, each family will be given materials and instructions for completing their own portion of the installation. For example, you might create an installation around *The Very Hungry Caterpillar* (Carle) where each family can complete specific parts of the story as pictures that then form the full story when displayed together in your space.

A program of this kind is best suited to an exciting event. A celebration of a particular author's birthday, for example, is an excellent time to schedule this program. Kicking off or wrapping up summer reading events would be another great time for a program like this. Marking a milestone in your community and celebrating an anniversary of your library building are other times this program would fit well in your series.

❖ POTENTIAL PITFALLS

Potential pitfalls with this project are surprisingly few, assuming you have found an excited and dedicated program provider. Your provider should be prepared to fill in gaps that may result from too few families attending the installation program. You should also prepare to assist families unsure about having their artwork displayed for all to see. One way to do this might be to invite your presenter to create outlines of the desired art for each family and then provide interesting materials for families to use to fill in the outlines. Taken together, these pieces would create a visually stimulating installation for all your library users to enjoy.

⌘ NEED TO DIY?

Flip over to the next chapter and take a look at our suggested Artwork Display Wall ongoing program series!

Health and Nutrition Programs

Health and nutrition are of paramount importance to children ages birth through preschool. Children experiencing malnourishment or regular hunger are simply not able to learn due to an inability to concentrate on learning tasks. And children do not simply need food: they need nutritious food filled with vitamins to ensure proper physical and mental development! Parents are looking for ways to incorporate healthy food options into their children's diet, and early learning programs focused on cooking and eating can provide excellent resources to accomplish this. Simultaneously, these programs can be a welcome resource for any family struggling to provide for their children.

Other health considerations are critical as well. Regular doctor and dentist checkups are important, but are often sources of anxiety for both children and parents. Other sources of anxiety include learning that a child needs assistance to meet developmental milestones. Health-focused programs in your early learning series will go far to alleviate some of the anxieties children and parents face when addressing these vital parts of development.

Cooking (without the Hot Appliances of Course!)

Cooking with this age group is a welcome activity, as it provides little ones a chance to scoop, measure, stir, and pour—all activities usually reserved for grown-ups! When we discuss a cooking program, we are not suggesting any hot appliances. Rather, we are referring to programs where little ones can assemble a healthy snack and then eat it with their caregivers!

Reaching out to professional cooking schools, healthy eating nonprofits, or even health food grocery stores will enable you to find a presenter for an early learning cooking class. Your presenter should be able to formulate a healthy recipe easy enough for children to assemble on their own! Ideally, presenters will also be prepared to discuss a couple of healthy eating tips while facilitating the program.

We have had success with cooking classes that center on fruit-based recipes and sandwich-like recipes. For example, we have assembled Watermelon Splits, where nutritious ingredients take the place of traditional Banana Split ingredients: large balls of watermelon instead of scoops of ice cream, vanilla yogurt instead of whipped cream, and a drizzle of honey instead of a drizzle of caramel sauce. Children love assembling their own concoction and learn plenty of self-control while scooping, measuring, and even drizzling. Incidentally, children in our early learning programs were delighted to make something they could then feed to their caregivers, rather than vice versa as is usually the case!

❖ POTENTIAL PITFALLS

The primary potential pitfall with this program is food allergies. We highly encourage a blanket policy of no nuts. Sunbutter is an excellent alternative to any sort of nut butter required for a recipe; otherwise, most recipes with nuts can simply be avoided. We also suggest providing an alternative to dairy, as that is another prevalent allergy. Nut butter yogurts and milks are easy enough to find, and having that option on hand is simply a good practice. Most importantly, we highly recommend publicizing your full ingredients list ahead of time and noting on all promotional material that caregivers should notify you or your instructor of any food allergies or aversions ahead of time. This will ensure that parents with the publicity materials have time to prepare in advance for a food-based early learning program.

⌘ NEED TO DIY?

It is possible! The aforementioned example of Watermelon Splits is a doable program on your own. You'll want to assemble ahead of time by gathering watermelons cut in half, an ice-cream scoop to divvy out the watermelons, a variety of fresh fruit (berries are always a hit), bananas, plastic knives or butter knives, cutting boards, bowls, and then vanilla yogurt, honey, and perhaps even mini chocolate chips for toppings. You'll begin by introducing families to the recipe and your method for how they will assemble Watermelon Splits. Then, turn your group loose on the ingredients! Encourage caregivers to allow children to scoop, cut, and mix, even if the result looks a bit icky. Your group will conclude the program by enjoying their treats together.

Eating

Cheese tasting anyone? Maybe even bring the goat?

A variation on a cooking class is an eating class! Both cooking and eating programs are excellent ways to address proper nutrition, as this is key to children being successful in school (and life!). These programs are also particularly helpful for disadvantaged families who would certainly appreciate access to free, healthy snacks for their children.

In our communities, we have a number of options for putting together food-based programs. A local cheese shop has plenty of curious snacks to try: various cheeses from goats, sheep, and cows, as well as dried fruits and fun bread and crackers. Another presenter for our programs creates, packages, and sells her own line of baby and toddler snacks. A third presenter is the owner of a local smoothie shop. We encourage you to think creatively about your community and what businesses might be interested in partnering with you to provide an early learning program on healthy eating. You might be surprised with what you come up with!

With these programs, we encourage you to plan to facilitate alongside your community business partner. Your role would be to introduce the types of food you all will be trying together and then present where these foods come from. Perhaps you are doing a cheese tasting and can provide a picture book of life on a farm, or with snacks and smoothies, the fruits and vegetables from which these are made. From here, your presenter will begin offering the food itself. We encourage you to distribute one item at a time and let your presenter's expertise shine here; go ahead and use big words, discuss the process, talk about the woes of added sugar, and so forth. Caregivers will appreciate these tidbits while children get to sample various tastes. We also encourage you to introduce new vocabulary about tastes and invite children to share what they think of each item as they taste it. A great way to wrap up this program is by inviting families to have a full snack sized portion of the foods they liked best!

If you would like to take this program concept up a notch, we encourage you to seek out the possibility of bringing in a presenter from a petting zoo. Some petting zoos allow animals to travel, and in this case, children would not only meet an animal that can provide food (such as milk and cheese), but also be able to interact with it! It may be worth noting that we are thinking of goats and lambs here, not cows! It may also worth noting that this part of your program would need an outdoor space to be successful.

❖ POTENTIAL PITFALLS

As with the previous program, the top potential pitfall here is food allergies. Publicizing clearly what will be served will enable your families to prepare in advance for this program. Again, we encourage no nuts. With dairy, we encourage you to have alternatives ready. For example, with the cheese tasting, *all* the families in the room might enjoy comparing a few vegan "cheeses" to traditional cheeses, and your families avoiding dairy will be able to stick to just those!

⌘ **NEED TO DIY?**

Good luck getting a goat to your library at the last minute! But, there are plenty of other ways to DIY this program without live farm animals. A quick look online plus a quick run to your nearest grocery store should enable you to provide a successful eating program. We suggest theming your program so that it makes sense to your families: all fruits, all vegetables, all chocolates, this sort of thing. You might have time to bring in a blender to make smoothies for everyone or even a juicer to make vegetable juice for your group. If you have ample time to prepare, you could borrow an ice-cream maker and churn out a batch of coconut-milk based ice cream topped with fruit or chocolate bits (or both!). Whatever food you decide to work with, simply stick with the structure of first introducing the food, then sampling, and then enjoying a full snack as a group!

Parent-Child Aerobics

Yes, toddler aerobics classes really do exist! This is a fun session, for everyone! These classes share some elements of movement programs but are a bit more involved and more health conscious.

You might find a presenter for this program at your nearest jazzercise studio, or you may already be in a community with a studio dedicated to toddler, or parent-child, aerobics classes. If neither option exists, you might approach your local recreation center to see if an instructor used to teaching children's lessons would be interested in developing this program for your early learning program series.

Aerobics programs for this age group involve the caregiver as much as, or perhaps even more than, the child! These programs are particularly fun because they often directly replicate common aerobics exercises from adult classes. These programs might also incorporate color recognition and language development if provided by an experienced instructor.

Often, these programs will include lively music, sometimes incorporating music that is fun and nostalgic to the adults present. The program will begin with warm-up stretches and exercises before moving into fun, physical literacy games for both children and caregivers. Adult participants should actually experience a slightly elevated heart rate once they get into the exercises, and children simply love to follow along with what their caregivers are doing. Step aerobics exercises usually form the backbone of this program, and alternating feet is an outstanding skill for little ones to practice. A fun conclusion to this program might be a lively group dance or parachute play. Instructors may provide a number of props, and caregivers might be encouraged to attend in loose, comfortable clothing.

❖ POTENTIAL PITFALLS

The obvious potential pitfall for this program is, of course, the possibility of injury. Instructors experienced providing these programs will have a number of ways to prevent this from happening. Still, toddlers and preschoolers, and especially new walkers, are less coordinated and therefore more prone to bonk and bump. Make sure each family has plenty of space to move around in and take quiet breathing breaks if (when?) the children become too wild with energy.

⌘ NEED TO DIY?

Grab your nearest exercise tape and push play! No, providing this program on your own is slightly more involved than that, but short exercise videos would be a great place to start your planning. We do not suggest trying to teach a full aerobics course, but rather put together a series of fun exercise games to play together. Stepping forward and back slowly, then moving quickly is a great place to start. Jumping jacks can be taught step-by-step, and then practiced all together as a group. Simple dance steps learned together in a large circle makes for an energetic activity, and if you have a parachute, some parachute playtime is a great way to wrap up.

Preparing for the Doctor

Yikes! An anxious event for both children and parents! Doctor visits are a necessary and nerve-wracking part of every child's life. Offering an early learning program to help children orient themselves to a visit to the doctor's office is incredibly helpful to both children and parents alike!

There are a number of places to look for a presenter for this program, but perhaps the best place is the nearest medical office complex or hospital! You'd want to work with your presenter to put together a program that allows children to explore the instruments they will see during a visit to the doctor. Since we can assume the doctor (or nurse) you are working with will not charge you to provide this program, we encourage you to spend your budget for this program on a small emergency medical kit for each family to take home!

This program will ideally begin with your presenter introducing herself, hopefully while dressed exactly as children would see a medical professional dressed in an actual doctor's office. The doctor will then introduce the various medical instruments he or she uses, probably a stethoscope, an otoscope, a blood pressure cuff, and a tongue depressor. (*Not* a syringe!) Ideally, your presenter will bring several of each and then invite each family to take turns trying each one out. Regardless, each child should have an opportunity to try out each instrument. Conclude your program by bringing out the first-aid materials children are used to seeing but most often not able to touch: thermometers and Band-Aids, for example. Children can then try each out on their caregivers, for a change! Hopefully, each of your families will also leave with a basic first-aid kit.

❖ POTENTIAL PITFALLS

The glaring potential pitfall of this program is children believing they will have to interact with an actual doctor in a way that is less than desirable. Many children are truly terrified of medical professionals. While this is obviously what this program is designed to address, getting children to feel comfortable in a room with a doctor may not be easy. Encourage parents to prepare children ahead of time for this program. Suggest the doctor sit right on the floor with the children, or have stethoscopes out for children as soon as they arrive to try out on parents or on the doctor! Be ready for some children to simply not be able to manage, and encourage those families to return at the end to play with the thermometers and Band-Aids and to take home a first-aid kit. If even that is too much, have some library books about doctor visits on hand, and send families with traumatized children home with one of those.

⌘ NEED TO DIY?

We doubt you can procure the medical instruments a doctor would bring for this program. That said, you could still pull this program off on your own. Instead of a doctor visiting, select a book about visiting a doctor, and read that with your group. Encourage children and caregivers to think of words that describe how they feel about going to the doctor. Then, provide thermometers and Band-Aids for the latter part of the program as described earlier, and still send families home with a first-aid kit. Even this DIY version will go a long way toward breaking down barriers of fear and trepidation many children experience about going to the doctor.

Developmental Play

Think occupational therapist suggested games! Many families with children this age are attending their very first parent-teacher conferences at daycares or preschools and learning how their children are excelling or how their children may need to improve in some areas. Even families with children too young for preschool are still experiencing visits with pediatricians looking for childhood development milestones. Any parent receiving information about how their child might need to improve in a developmental area may experience anxiety and uncertainty as to what to do next. An early learning program with an occupational therapist will enable parents with children of *all* abilities to learn simple games and tasks children can practice to meet developmental milestones.

Either an occupational therapist or a family psychologist would be an excellent presenter for this program. Play therapists are also able to present a program of this kind. Invite your presenter to think of the topmost milestones for children ages birth through preschool, perhaps about five to six milestones. Then ask him or her to bring along one to two activities that will encourage children working toward meeting those milestones.

For this program, your occupational therapist will ideally sit on the floor along with your families. He or she will present each milestone and then the activities for children to practice meeting that milestone. Ideally, the therapist will bring several sets of each activity, and children can take turns practicing each one. Your presenter is already an expert in these areas and is sure to have a plan for presenting to a group of families at once. Your program will most likely conclude with all activities out and all children practicing one or more on repeat. Parents will likely have a number of questions during this program, and an unrehearsed, Q&A format is usually the best one when presenting on these topics.

❖ POTENTIAL PITFALLS

One potential pitfall with this program is it being inadvertently triggering for parents. Parents with children facing developmental challenges may be disheartened or discouraged seeing their child struggle while others succeed. Your professional presenter will know the right verbiage to use with parents, regardless of their child's abilities. Your positive encouragement throughout this program will also go a long way toward all caregivers feeling like their experience was successful. Being sure your presenter is prepared to answer follow-up questions on an individual basis will also help uncertain parents feel comfortable with their experience that day.

⌘ NEED TO DIY?

We suggest you skip over the professional elements of this program and focus instead on activities that help meet developmental milestones. Activities that encourage sorting, pinching, balancing, and stacking are all easy, doable places to start. Many can be done with supplies you likely already have on hand or with no supplies at all! Set up your program space with five to six different activities, and ask families to take turns trying each one. You might introduce the program with a quick sentence on what milestone each activity is designed to help meet, but we suggest leaving the in depth lingo there. Focus instead on your families having a fun experience practicing each of the different activities. Manage your group by allowing about five minutes per station, and then asking everyone to switch, thus ensuring each family can practice each activity at least one time.

Wellness Programs

Libraries are becoming increasingly more critical to the well-being of society as a whole. Despite the fact that social work is not a required class in library school (yet), librarians often find themselves providing comfort and resources to adults who are experiencing homelessness, families living on the poverty line, and children and teenagers who may not have stable homes or who are struggling to succeed in school for various reasons. As one of the last bastions of social wellness in the community, it is becoming a library's obligation in some cases to be able to provide experiences for its customers that promote socioemotional wellness to bring peace and calm to a person, a home, or the community.

Yoga

Yoga serves a variety of purposes for families. On the very surface level, it is an opportunity for families to move through poses, strengthen their bodies, and improve their flexibility. As we go deeper, however, there are many more benefits to just such a program.

First, yoga involves the use of a mat. This mat is a child's space for the duration of the program. Some children may or may not have access to a space that is uniquely theirs very often during the day, and having this space can create a sense of calm for that child that may not otherwise be able to be achieved. It can help soothe overactivity and encourage creative exploration of movement in a safe space. Second, breathing is one of the most critical ways of soothing human emotion. An example that was used in one of our yoga classes was when the instructor provided a piece of yarn for each participant, about six to eight inches in length. The instructor asked families to hold that string up in front of their faces and to take a deep breath, exhaling in such a way as to make the piece of yarn move. This activity immediately demands focus: to bring the attention of the child or caregiver to the piece of yarn. Second, if the person holding the string is struggling to exhale in more than ragged breaths, this helps them to lengthen those exhalations which is a soothing component in itself. Each participant was invited to keep their piece of yarn as a free, light, and small tool to keep in their purse or diaper bag to use when things got tough for them or their children.

Yoga is widely provided in many communities, with a variety of providers available and willing to do programs such as these. It is advised to hire someone who is a certified yogi because while the poses done with children may not be complex, these people have been trained in proper alignment and implementation and can assist with problems if they arise.

❖ POTENTIAL PITFALLS

A potential pitfall is that your families may or may not have access to yoga mats to use for the program. If your library has the budget, purchasing a set to keep at the library for these programs is an excellent investment, particularly as you repeat these programs. If not, families can bring towels or blankets instead to use to demarcate their space on the floor.

⌘ NEED TO DIY?

If you are not a certified yoga instructor, we advise against doing poses that would risk injury to child or caregiver. However, there are several poses that can be used safely for the nature of this program. Telling a story with your bodies is an excellent introduction to movement through yoga. An excellent book to use is *Early Bird* by Toni Yuly. In this book, Early Bird rises early to greet the day (because as we all know, the early bird gets the worm!). However, the story does not end exactly as one would expect. The book utilizes simple phrases that translate easily into yoga poses. Mountain Pose, cat/cow, and cobra pose are accessible for children and families and can also be incorporated into this story. There are many tutorials that can be found on DVDs in the library's collection and online to assist with this process. You can read the story together once and then tell the story again through yoga poses.

Mindfulness and Meditation

When we picture toddlers, the idea of mindfulness and meditation may seem quite contrary to the energy with which they tend to approach life. This, however, is precisely why a mindfulness and meditation program is an asset to your early learning program series. From a very early age, we can begin to practice techniques that enable us to invite calm when we feel chaotic and to manage our emotions and consequently our actions. Teaching babies, toddlers, and preschoolers some of these techniques is advantageous for them and for their caregivers. These techniques will also help young children be successful when confronted with the myriad of emotions preschool and kindergarten are likely to trigger.

If you have not practiced mindfulness and meditation with children, you may be surprised to learn what a program on these practices might look like! Programs do not require children to sit with hands on knees, eyes closed, and humming. Rather, these programs will work through a series of exercises that invite children and caregivers to experience body awareness and mental control.

Mindfulness and meditation programs are best facilitated by a meditation instructor, ideally one with experience working with children. If you are unable to find this individual to present your program, seek out a children's yoga instructor instead.

Your program will likely begin with your presenter orienting caregivers to what to expect during the program and what not to expect. Presenters may bring meditation cushions, yoga mats, and/or coloring sheets to aid in their exercises. They may play soothing music or nature sounds at times or soft musical instruments. On the whole, though, the program will work through a series of kid-friendly mental and physical exercises that simply build awareness of the self.

One such exercise invites children to picture a pond with five different fish. Each fish is given a different color, which the children help predict, based on his or her emotional state. One fish is angry, one is scared, one is happy, and so on. Children are invited to demonstrate each of these emotions while selecting the best color to picture representing each emotion. Then, children are asked to visualize being the water, rather than one of the fish. Caregivers are instructed that such an exercise invites children to observe their feelings, rather than giving into them and acting out of them.

Your program will most likely conclude with a group-led, quiet breathing exercise. Your presenter may even bring stuffed animals to act as breathing buddies or breathing friends; children will be asked to lie down with their breathing friend on their tummy, and use their breath to make their breathing friend rise and fall in a relaxing manner.

❖ POTENTIAL PITFALLS

One potential pitfall with this program is discomfort about the idea of meditating. While many families embrace this concept, others have negative connotations with it. A skilled presenter will quickly put your families at ease by inviting them to participate up to the level they feel comfortable participating. Once families experience the first exercise, they generally see that this is an accessible concept rather than a difficult one and are happy continuing with the program as planned.

⌘ NEED TO DIY?

As with yoga, we suggest you avoid the professional instruction aspects of this program. If you are presenting on your own, you might seek out one of many books for children on mindfulness. These books offer guided exercises, and sometimes corresponding yoga poses, that you can explore with your group. From there, you might find one to two worksheets that encourage mindfulness and print enough copies for your group. Supply crayons for the children to color as you read the mindfulness practice associated with each worksheet. You might conclude with the breathing friend exercise outlined earlier, or if you are more comfortable, a gratitude practice. For this, allow each child or caregiver (or both!) to name one thing for which he or she is grateful. Have a stack of cards, and write the name of each thing on a card as it is shared with you. A particularly nice idea for these cards is to have them be the start of a gratitude jar you place in the children's section of your library, to which other families might contribute. Or, simply make a huge stack of the wonderful things we are thankful for, and end your program by thanking your participants for their attendance.

Essential Oils and Aromatherapy

A program on aromatherapy might seem as unlikely a choice as a meditation program for an early learning program series. But like mindfulness and meditation techniques, essential oils and aromatherapy can be welcome tools in families needing to help young children manage a myriad of emotions.

Aromatherapy is not only an excellent tool for inviting calmness and peacefulness: a program on aromatherapy will explore essential oils that awaken, enliven, and invite joy, as well. Other essential oils have been known to clear congestion, soothe muscle aches, and boost immunity.

A skilled herbalist in your community would be an excellent presenter of a program like this. Many yoga instructors have a basic knowledge of essential oils and could also provide such a program. You will likely work closely with this presenter to develop the program you want for your series. Some program participants might eagerly embrace a session on this topic, while others may approach with skepticism or even concern. Including two important tidbits at the outset will help frame your program well: the first is that essential oils are not for everyone and that you (and your presenter) are not prescribing anything to anyone, but rather are exploring possibilities. The second is that you are all there to learn, not to heal wounds and treat illnesses. Approaching this program as a learning experience will encourage both children and caregivers alike to have an open mind and be there to explore new things rather than to judge them.

Like a mindfulness and mediation program, an early learning program on aromatherapy may be different from what you would expect! After the aforementioned introduction, the presenter will likely produce small bottles of essential oils with child-safe tops to pass around and smell. These will be limited in number. It will be fun for your participants to attempt to guess what smell they think is in each bottle! An experienced presenter may even produce the plant or fruit (such as lavender or mandarin orange) from which the oil came. Children will then be invited to create one or more aromatherapy products to take home. These may range from scented "magic" wands that children can spritz with certain scents that invite courage or bravery. Or, these may be room spritzers that children can take home to use as needed.

Caregivers play a key role in this program, as they determine what scents will fit best for their families. Since working with essential oils is a delicate process, each activity may take up to 10 or even 15 minutes each. The general atmosphere during a program of this nature is calm and peaceful, even quiet, and the process of concocting together is often a very sweet experience for children and caregivers.

Once the essential oils projects are completed, we suggest concluding this program with a very accessible activity to ensure that anyone uncertain about the oils still leaves feeling accomplished. This might be as simple as adding decorations to the spritzer bottles or as complex as potting a small lavender plant to take home. We also suggest having your presenter provide a quick guide handout to the oils discussed, including safety tips for using these oils at home with children. Any experienced herbalist will be more than equipped to provide this information for parents to take home!

❖ POTENTIAL PITFALLS

Potential pitfalls with this program center on the oils themselves. As mentioned already, some families may be reluctant to attend a session on aromatherapy. Presenting this as an exploratory program will help alleviate concerns. Alternately, some families may approach this program looking for healing remedies, even for specific medical concerns. Stating clearly that this program is not medical advice will help set appropriate expectations. In addition to these possible scenarios, you may experience children not being able to manage the oils carefully, which could even result in a spill. Most program presenters will prepare in advance by having safety caps on their bottles of oils, which ensure that only a few drops might leave the bottle at a time. But, being prepared for a spill is nonetheless a wise idea. For this reason, you might suggest that presenters bring the less-expensive oils in their lineup to avoid this program being more costly than planned!

⌘ NEED TO DIY?

You can! Lavender is a very approachable essential oil, and you could design an early learning program around this one scent. You might begin the program with lavender lotion, and as you greet each family, ask if they would like a squirt to rub into their skin. Then, you could provide supplies to make the aforementioned magic wands. These could be somewhat standard, with a small dowel and many decoration options, or you could embrace the natural world by providing a collection of sticks and using yarn or ribbon to add whimsical streamers to each. You can instruct children that these wands, when spritzed with the calming lavender scent, can be used to "magically" ward off scary feelings and invite peaceful ones instead, *or* can be used anytime, with any scent, just for fun! If you want to add a second activity, it is possible to create spritzers with your families. You will need supplies in advance from your local health food store. A knowledgeable store associate will be able to help you find small spritzer bottles, a carrier oil, and lavender essential oil. You could conclude your DIY version of this program with one or two tips for caregivers. For example, a small spritzer is nice to have on hand. A parent might spray a bit into the air near an upset child and invite the child to take a big whiff. Even if the scent itself has no effect whatsoever, at least the anxious child has just managed to take a big, deep breath!

Social-Emotional Skills

A great way to conclude, since truly these opportunities are a part of every program! Increasing importance is being placed upon social-emotional skills in school settings, and one of the topmost buzzwords within this skill set is *empathy*. While all early learning programs in this lineup provide opportunities to practice varied social-emotional skills such as self-regulation and listening to others, we do also want to include a program suggestion specifically focused on developing empathy.

Empathy begins with an open-mindedness that then allows an individual to engage in compassionate behavior and view a situation with a broadened perspective. We developed the idea of offering an entire early learning program in an unfamiliar language, but with familiar activities, to immerse children and caregivers in an environment that requires open-mindedness to be successful.

Finding a presenter for this program might be relatively easy, as many community members speak more than one language and identify with the culture that speaks that language. In our case, we developed a French storytime.

An ideal program of this type will use zero English in its presentation. Children and caregivers will be led through a traditional storytime in a new language. We suggest that your presenter read books children are already familiar with, translated into the language you are presenting. Add songs with movements that your participants are asked to follow along with, and perhaps offer snacks from the country in which this language is spoken. Assure your families that this is for fun, and it is just to try. To conclude, try singing a familiar song together, in the language being presented.

❖ POTENTIAL PITFALLS

The potential pitfall with this program is that it truly feels uncomfortable. Hearing a language that is completely foreign and being asked to participate without understanding exactly what is being asked is a difficult situation to navigate. While you want to create this immersive environment to fulfill the goal of this program, making the program *too* inaccessible will only undermine your goal. Therefore, we suggest that while your presenter uses only the language he or she has decided to present in, you encourage your families in English throughout the program. Model following along with song motions even without being able to pronounce, and jump in with a "let's try it!" when you feel your families might be confused or discouraged. Ask your presenter to plan to teach three color words (red, yellow, and blue perhaps) and three number words (one, two, and three) in this alternate language, and have them repeat those words many times throughout the program with your participants echoing. This will leave everyone feeling somewhat successful. And concluding with a familiar song in this alternate language, even if it is not *exactly* culturally representative, will still go far to end your program on a positive note.

⌘ NEED TO DIY?

You probably can, even if you are not bilingual! It is likely that you already know someone who speaks more than one language and that person may even be on your library staff! You are more than capable of putting together a traditional storytime, and then sharing that plan with a copresenter who can translate it into their second (or first!) language. The overall goal of this program is introducing young children to an environment that requires open-mindedness, much like preschool and kindergarten will require of them on a regular basis.

IN SUMMARY

While our actual program plans with presenters are obviously quite detailed, we intentionally presented these programming ideas to you as suggestions for a direction in which you might take each program topic. We hope that you are able to use our outline as the backbone of your early learning program series planning, allowing your presenters' creativity, and your own, to formulate specific programs that reflect the interests and needs of your community.

We encourage you to use all of these ideas as jumping-off points for your program series. We hope that you will try each at least once, as we know that varied experiences are key to early childhood learning. At the same time, we know that repetition is also key to learning and hope that you will find a way to repeat some of these programs at least one time during the course of a year. You might experiment with repeating favorite and popular programs and simply changing the content; for example, we often repeat our animal programs, but with different animals. Or, we will repeat our yoga programs with different stories to support the yoga. You may find that a program series will work well with your group, such as a full month working on learning basic ukulele chords, or a five-part visual arts program lineup. You will likely experience some programs, such as movement programs, working well with larger groups while others, such as aromatherapy, working better with smaller groups.

Most exciting, you will almost certainly develop your own early learning programs that differ from those on this list and perfectly represent your library community while fulfilling the overarching goal of your early learning program series: offering all families in your community access to play-based early learning experiences.

The following chapter will offer another set of 26 early learning program options. These will be presented in a more-detailed format than the open-ended ideas in this chapter, as it is most likely you will be planning and presenting the next 26 programs yourself.

YOUR TO-DO LIST

- Determine your budget.
- Identify community partners and business owners interested in providing programming.
- Sketch out a calendar based on program categories (i.e., each month will offer a movement program, a music program, etc.).
- Slot in program providers based on availability.
- Request payments for program providers according to your institution's practices.
- Put together publicity for your program series.
- Secure items needed for DIY backup plans.
- Get ready to have fun!

FOUR

Early Learning Programs for Tiny or Nonexistent Budgets

After reading the previous chapter, you may be feeling particularly excited about the types of programming available to you in your community or reflecting specifically on how your library can team up with other organizations to create new and unique opportunities for your library users. Alternatively, you may be feeling somewhat discouraged by the limited budget your library has to work with, especially if this is your first attempt at a program like Little University.

Have no fear! This chapter is all about what *you* can do at your library using the resources and skills available to you already. While it may seem like these take a little more effort on the ground, the work you put into the program whether you have a budget or not will reflect in its outcome. We promise that you can provide meaningful learning opportunities, and your Little University attendees will notice and appreciate the benefits they receive from your program no matter what size budget you happen to have.

In the following pages, we are including 26 of our most popular programs that we have executed with little to no money. As in the previous chapter, this will permit you to fill out an entire year of programming using these ideas, if you wish. Repetition is critical to learning for this age group, so once you have done a program one time, know that you can repeat it again with excellent results. And as the program provider, you will have the opportunity to learn from any pitfalls that occur the first time to make the next time even better.

TINY BUDGETS AS AN OPPORTUNITY

Budgets can be an enormous hurdle for libraries, especially when beginning to implement new types of programs. Many times, it can be most helpful for libraries to begin with programs that cost little to nothing to prove to those holding the purse strings that their programs are valid and can be successful on their own but can be even more successful with increased financial support. As the success of these programs becomes more tangible and measurable, the programs themselves appear more valid in the eyes of those who may not experience them directly. For several years, we both operated with extremely limited budgets for our programs and learned ways to provide meaningful programs for our library users that required little to no money.

Though it can seem hard or nearly impossible to operate fledgling programs with little to no money, with the right support and planning, librarians can create meaningful programs without additional funding. Doing so stretches the creative mind-set of the librarians and also models to parents and caregivers that early learning experiences can take place in the home as well, even when their own budgets are tight.

Try not to think of money as the only way to provide successful programming for your library users. Librarians not only know a lot themselves, but they also have access to intellectual resources across the Internet and through fellow librarians. Together, we are a robust community and can encourage and support one another from afar with the simple click of a button.

Also, children and education provide strong leverage when working with community partners for programming or other tangible, inexpensive gifts. With a little bit of imagination and the heart behind the mission, there is often more that can be achieved than at first meets the eye.

DIY PROGRAMMING EXAMPLES AND RESOURCES

Movement Programs

Librarians do not have to be experts in dance or yoga to put together a successful movement-based program for children and their families. As mentioned in the previous chapter, all programs for children should be focused more on the process than on the product, so sometimes when the person leading the program is less adept themselves, families feel more comfortable embracing that process component. Movements that involve gross motor skills build muscle strength and dexterity, improve health, and increase the number of neurons firing in a child's brain. As studies have shown, when a child is moving, he or she is learning.

As a quick side note here, this is a great piece of encouragement to give to families in any program, not just Little University. If you are in a story-time, for example, and one or more of your young attendees are having trouble sitting still, remind parents that learning looks different for every-one and that movement is not disrespectful to you. More often than not, parents will return to you at a subsequent program raving about how their child sang one of your storytime songs in the bathtub or at naptime, prov-ing that they really were paying attention even though the parent did not initially recognize that fact.

Bubbles

There is something about bubbles that gets children excited. Even dogs get excited about them! The ephemeral nature of bubbles is perhaps part of the joy they bring, in addition to being inexpensive, accessible, and mess-less.

With small children, it is especially important to discuss safety when it comes to programs like these. Little University requires adults and chil-dren to learn together, so giving bubbles to the parents is one way to improve the safety and enjoyment of the program. Additionally, children are likely to compete over getting to pop the bubbles, without paying atten-tion to who or what may lie before or around them. If you can find them, individual bubble wands are the most sanitary and engaging for families (dollar stores usually have a plethora in the spring and summer months). If you decide to go this route, it is ideal to have one wand per parent or per family for safety and health reasons. Families may even have some extras at home that they could donate if you put out a flyer at your circulation desk requesting them.

If purchasing individual bubble juice bottles is not in your budget, bub-ble machines can be a good way to prevent competition, especially because they create a huge number of bubbles in a short amount of time, without breaths having to be taken to refuel. While these machines can be expen-sive if one does not already exist in your library, they can be used again and again, so they may make a reasonable argument for purchase. This is another instance where you might be able to tap into your community to see if you can borrow one of these from another library user or see if someone wants to donate it to your program.

Toddler Prom

This is a program that several libraries have done recently, garnering a great deal of attention on social media. It serves both to encourage dancing to music while being dressed up and to enhance the "cute factor" of these types of programs.

1. **Attire**: Encourage both the children and the caregivers to dress up. Whether that means wearing an Elsa dress, a Spiderman suit, or honest-to-goodness formal wear, all forms of expression should be welcome.

   An additional bonus here, especially if you have a mix of income levels in your community, is to encourage a clothing swap to take place before or after the program. If families have clothes (especially dressier clothes in the interest of this program) that their children have outgrown, others might find them useful and be able to stretch their own budgets a little further by being able to reuse these in their own homes.

2. **Decorations**: Even just a bit of crepe paper and a few balloons can transform a space from one that was familiar to something more special. If you have teen volunteers at your library, they are an excellent resource for decorating for events like these. They will not only have the time to help, but giving them the chance to be creative in this way can bring even more ages of library user into the world of Little University.

3. **Music**: Digital music players, CD players, and Internet-based music platforms all offer easy ways to access music and are easy to use to create playlists. Adding a mix of music from different cultures and time periods bring together multiple generations and cultural backgrounds while providing impetus to move and explore the music.

Execution

1. When everyone arrives, welcome them and have them put any clothing or bags to the side of the room. There should be a dance floor clearly marked in the space so that everyone knows where is the safe space to have a break and where is the best place to get in on the action.

2. You can announce the party: "Welcome to Toddler Prom 2018!" and invite parents to take pictures of and dance with their children (just make sure to adhere to any privacy policies your library might have with regard to taking pictures of children).

3. Let the party begin! Press "play" on your awesome playlist and dance it up with your families (it is especially cool if library staff are able to participate in the dressing up as well to make the event more special for everyone). Guide participants through group dances and encourage creative movement on the more free-form songs.

4. Have water available (or punch/juice boxes if they are in your budget) for people to enjoy while taking breaks from the action.

5. Mixing in some slow songs can make for cute parent-child bonding time while also preventing things from getting too out of control. As mentioned in the previous chapter, it is important to have this change in mood to help regulate emotions and keep everyone safe.

6. Thank everyone for coming as they are leaving the program.

7. This program may naturally last longer than the 30-minute time frame we recommend for Little University programs. If it is possible in your library space and if your families are still having fun, feel free to carry things past the 30-minute mark. As people start getting tired, though, offering slower music and opportunities to wind down will be particularly important.

Disco Dance Party

Some libraries have access to a disco ball, and this can be a fun addition to any dance party. If there are librarians or other staff who play instruments, invite them to participate and provide music for the party. Live music can be a welcome novelty and can blend well with recorded songs.

Like Toddler Prom, children can be invited to wear costumes to this program, and dances can be taught (think things like the Electric Slide or the chicken dance) that parents may recognize and children will find fun and easy to replicate. Again, even if you are not an expert in any of these dances, the Internet can help you learn them (as can many of your program attendees!).

Set up the room in a similar way to Toddler Prom to add to the excitement of the program. If you are using a disco ball, make sure to add a disclaimer on the promotional flyer in case anyone may be sensitive to the flashing lights that it creates. If a family does have such a sensitivity, ask them if its presence alone is ok or if it should not be in the room at all and adjust accordingly.

Execution

1. When everyone arrives, welcome them and have them put any clothing or bags to the side of the room. There should be a dance floor clearly marked in the space so that everyone knows where is a safe space to have a break and where is the best place to get in on the action.

2. You can announce the party: "Welcome to our disco dance party!" and invite parents to take pictures of and dance with their children (as mentioned earlier, just make sure to adhere to any privacy policies your library might have in regards to taking pictures of children).

3. Let the party begin! Press "play" on your awesome playlist and dance it up with your families (it is especially cool if library staff are able to participate in the dressing up as well to make the event more special for everyone). Guide participants through group dances and encourage creative movement on the more free-form songs. Since it is a Disco Dance party, throw in some standard disco moves (you can look these up online if you are not familiar with many of them) to add some humor and authenticity to the program. These movements build gross motor skills and many of them cross the midline, an important component of early learning growth!

4. Like for Toddler Prom, have water available (or punch/juice boxes if they are in your budget) for people to enjoy while taking breaks from the action.

5. Mixing in some slow songs can make for cute parent-child bonding time while also preventing things from getting too out of control. As mentioned in the previous chapter, it is important to have this change in mood to help regulate emotions and keep everyone safe.

6. Thank everyone for coming as they are leaving the program.

7. This program may naturally last longer than the 30-minute time frame we recommend for Little University programs. If it is possible in your library space and if your families are still having fun, feel free to carry things past the 30-minute mark. As people start getting tired, though, offering slower music and opportunities to wind down will be particularly important.

Obstacle Course

To change things up a bit, creating an obstacle course for children can be an inexpensive and enjoyable learning opportunity.

- Take several objects that already exist in your library, from chairs to blocks to paper to books, and place them on the floor. Use tape or some other marker to help participants get from one point to the next in the order you prefer and to prevent bottlenecking or unintended bumper car-like impacts.

- Each station can have pictorial directions, allowing users to understand what to do at each one even if English is not a primary language. Do you hop three times on the yellow circle? Do you move in a circle clockwise around a chair? Use your imagination to develop what to do at each station, including movements that vary from one to the next. Programs like this help with balance, self-regulation, and important preschool skills like following directions and taking turns.

- If you were particularly intrigued by the tumbling program mentioned in the previous chapter, this can be an alternative to that program in a DIY setting. Having people progress through the stations in this program builds life skills like patience while also encouraging development through the execution of each specific movement.

Action Storytimes

Action storytimes are an excellent way to introduce a movement-based program to a group of participants already familiar with a storytime setting. At the same time, though, action storytimes are a fantastic way to bring a literacy component into your early learning program series. Action storytime centers on movement with books being used to prompt the sequence of movements.

- Choose five to six picture books (you will be reading these quickly!) that require, or suggest, action while reading. *We're Going on a Bear Hunt* by Michael Rosen is a classic, but many others are available as well. Eric Carle's *From Head to Toe* is a great go-to option. Many of Jan Thomas' books are both hilarious and action oriented. Or, any number of books featuring animals will invite actions mimicking animal behaviors and gaits.

- As the facilitator, you will read through these books one to two sentences at a time, modeling the action that corresponds to each page. Then, your participants will join you in repeating that action. It gets raucous and lively fast, so be ready!

- Consider ending with a book that is participatory but does not require action. For example, Jane Calbrea's books invite singing along, with possible lap-sit motions added, but do not encourage gross motor movements. This conclusion will help wind your participants down from the high energy levels an action storytime creates!

Mind-Body Coordination Games

Similar to action storytimes but much quieter and calmer, this early learning program uses books to prompt yoga poses and breathing exercises.

- Select three to four picture books (you will read these at a slower pace) based on yoga movements and mindfulness activities. *I Am Yoga* (Peter Reynolds, illustrator) or *Yoga Bunny* (Brian Russo) are excellent books to introduce the concept of the program. *Good Morning Yoga* or *Good Night Yoga* would be great second books (or have both on hand!) as they go more in-depth. *My Magic Breath* (Alison Taylor) is an excellent choice for a conclusion.

- As noted earlier, you will be facilitating this program largely by demonstrating the poses and activities suggested by the book. That said, each page gives clear, succinct instructions as to what pose is being suggested. Simply follow along with what the book says, being aware of the importance of demonstrating for any families who find English instructions unclear.

- Your final book should invite children to sit together with their caregivers and practice deep breathing, an excellent way to find calm—for *both* children and caregivers—during tricky toddler and preschool years.

Art and Craft Programs

Loose Parts Painting Parties

Materials

- Sturdy paper, at least two sheets per child.
- Tempera paint: we suggest only providing red, yellow, and blue, as the colors will mix on the child's artwork and naturally create orange, green, and purple (and brown). Color mixing will be a part of the learning experience.

- Found objects: anything a child could use as a stamp will work perfectly. Try old Duplos, cut up cleaning sponges; really, anything goes. You could also cut up vegetables such as potatoes and celery.
- Table covers to help with the mess.
- Paper plates to put dollops of paint on.
- Ideally, bits of masking tape to hold each child's paper to the table cover.

Process

1. Start the program with a visual example. Have your participants crowd around to watch you use each found object as a stamp or paintbrush to create a picture on a piece of paper.
2. Now send the children off to create!

    - Zero- to two-year-olds are most likely to use this as an opportunity to finger paint. Allowing them to explore this way is a wonderful idea and a beautiful way to encourage their fine motor development. If parents appear disconcerted, provide them the second sheet of paper toward the end of the program to make a nice painting of their baby's handprints.

    - Two- to four-year-olds are very likely to get the concept of this program immediately. This age group will most likely spend the bulk of the program time making an extraordinary mess on their paper. As mentioned earlier, offer the second sheet of paper toward the end of the program, and invite these children to create a simpler picture to take home.

    - Four- to five-year-olds will likely ask for a paintbrush. Encourage them to think creatively about how to use the found objects as paintbrushes. This will stretch their imaginations as well as strengthen their fine motor control. Again, you will be able to offer them a second sheet of paper to create a take-home piece of artwork.

Marble Art Greeting Cards

Materials

All you need for this program to be successful are shallow boxes with sides (tops of paper boxes work perfectly for this program), marbles, cardstock paper, crayons, and paint (washable tempera is a great option).

Encourage families to wear older clothes for this program in the event that a marble strays from its box and lands on an unsuspecting victim. If you have paint smocks (or old T-shirts from another program) make these available to families, as well.

Process

1. Start the program with the cardstock paper and write a message inside with the crayons provided. Depending on the age of the child, this message will look different:

    *   Zero- to two-year-olds will likely do more scribbling than writing, although individual letters may be starting to form. These scribbles are critical to improving the fine motor skills needed for writing, so allow them the freedom to create as they can and will. If the card is going to a friend or relative, grown-ups can feel free to "interpret" the scribble after it is completed.

    *   Three- to four-year-olds will be more capable of forming letters, often those of their own name. If they are at this point, that is great. If they are not quite there, scribbling, like for the younger children, is equally important.

    *   Four- to five-year-olds, especially those preparing for kindergarten, may have even more writing skills. Encourage each level to participate in this part of the program to the best of their abilities and again remind parents that this, like everything in Little University, is about the *process* more than the *product*.

2. Now comes the fun part—painting!

    *   Place the cardstock on the bottom of the box lid, making sure that the scribbles that were made previously are face down and there is a blank canvas to work with.

    *   Invite parents to help children place blobs of paint to the side of the cardstock in whatever colors they like.

    *   Next, add marbles. Depending on how many marbles you have, each child can have anywhere from one to five. This is a moment to take a pause and talk to everyone about the safety of working with these materials. They are very small and can cause choking hazards for young children. Parents need to be alert to ensure that these marbles remain in the box lid for the purposes of painting and to quickly capture any that stray from the box.

- Grown-ups can help children manipulate the marbles in the box in much the same way as a miner would pan for gold. Holding onto the edges, participants will tip the box from side to side and corner to corner, allowing the marbles to track over the blobs of paint and then across the cardstock, creating an abstract masterpiece.

- Continue in this way as long as desired, and then return all materials to a table or other designated space. If there is space to hang or lay the cards out to dry, invite parents to leave them while they finish whatever other activities they had planned at the library that day. Otherwise, families should take their finished products with them as they leave.

Artwork Display Walls

No matter the size of your library, big or small, there is a good chance that there is some manner of wall space that is not being used. Take advantage of this by offering a program to beautify it in the spirit of Little University!

Materials

- Paper. Any kind will work for this depending on your end goal. Do you want a banner? Butcher block is great for that purpose. Will there be individual papers? A selection of coloring pages or scrap paper from elsewhere in the library work well. You can do this however makes most sense in your community!

- Writing utensils. Markers, crayons, pens, colored pencils, chalk—you get the idea. No matter the end result, holding these in little hands builds writing skills!

Process

1. Have all materials out for families at the beginning of the program. As we have mentioned before, having the room set up in advance adds to the professional feel of the program and helps encourage self-regulation as families must wait to use any of them.

2. Explain the purpose of the program: to beautify the library, introduce others to Little University, and build writing skills. If you have a specific additional desire, like creating a community banner around a theme, this is the time to explain that, as well.

3. Let people create! Having instrumental music playing in the background can get creative juices flowing and stimulate brain activity around the drawing and writing.

4. Allow attendees several pieces of paper, if possible, inviting them to make the first one (or several) for the library and another to take home.

5. After the program, hang up the pictures (if appropriate, participants can help with this).

6. A passive addition or alternative to this program is to put out the materials in the children's section of the library with a sign explaining the project and inviting more participation. You may want to start an online or physical "portfolio" for projects as they cycle off of the display wall, making room for more!

Toilet Paper Roll Bird Feeders

Materials

*   Toilet paper rolls or similar.
*   Sunbutter: plan for one jar of sunbutter per table, or one jar of sunbutter per four families. You can find sunbutter at health food stores, or you can make your own by pulverizing sunflower seeds in a blender until they become the consistency of peanut butter. (Alternately, you *can* just use peanut butter for this—we just avoid nuts with all of our early learning programs due to possible allergies!)
*   Sunflower seeds.
*   Millet.
*   Cracked corn, or dried corn.
*   Quinoa.
*   Dried fruit: we suggest raisins as they are the least expensive.
*   Cups to scoop, if you have them. (These are not necessary as children can use their hands, but can help regulate the scooping process if available.)
*   A big plastic tub for mixing the birdseed, and ideally one smaller tub per table to divide up the birdseed.
*   Butter knives or plastic knives.
*   Table covers (old newspapers also work).

- Hole punch.
- String or twine.
- Ideally, pictures of birds eating out of bird feeders (for children unfamiliar with the concept of a bird feeder—you would be surprised!).

Process

1. Have the pictures available to pass around or look at together to orient children to the concept of what you are making during this early learning program.

2. Begin by making birdseed together. Have children take turns scooping out the birdseed ingredients into your big tub. It does not matter how much of each ingredient is added (birds are not picky!), but be aware to make sure the mixture includes more dry ingredients than fruit, as it will be easier to work with this way.

3. Once the birdseed is assembled, send the families off to your tables to start the rest of the process. They will first punch two holes on opposite sides of one end of the toilet paper roll to use as anchors for hanging up their bird feeder later.

4. Children will then coat the toilet paper roll in sunbutter. The easiest and the most fun way to do this is with their hands. Children unsure of this, though, might prefer using a butter knife or plastic knife for this step. Either way, this step is the fine motor skills moment of the day!

5. Then, children will roll their sunbutter-covered toilet paper roll through the birdseed tub until it is covered (or mostly covered) in birdseed.

6. Caregivers will help with the final step, which is threading the twine or string through the holes in the toilet paper roll and tying it so that the bird feeder can hang from a balcony ceiling or tree branch when taken home.

7. If you have the time and supplies, families generally appreciate making more than one of these, as children learn through repetition and will likely want to repeat the process once they have mastered the steps in the first attempt. Alternately, families can conclude the program by helping you make hand-formed birdseed balls out of the leftover sunbutter and birdseed. These could be placed outside your library branch or taken home by your families. (Birdseed balls will most likely be snatched up by squirrels when placed outside, but the point here is the fine motor skills rather than bird-watching!)

Community Programs and Destination Storytimes

Nearly every profession in existence requires the use of reading and writing in order for people to be successful at it. Everyone from doctors to lawyers to construction workers to zookeepers need to be able to read and comprehend instructions in order to do their jobs well. When these community partners find their way into the library and take time out of their busy schedules to read to children and impress upon them the importance of learning to read, it makes a difference in the lives of those children and their families. People like firefighters and policemen, especially, make an impact because they are people children can see on a regular basis and can then connect with the positive event they experienced with them at the library.

Firefighters

Firefighters may have one of the most glamorous jobs in the world in the eyes of a young child. As the sirens come blaring down the street, children immediately recognize the sound and may point and say "fire truck!" in exuberance as it drives by. One of the goals firefighters have is to connect with the community and build positive relationships when they are not out fighting fires or responding to emergencies in the area. They are often very friendly and easy to work with and, in our experience, have been ready and willing to read with children. If you decide that firefighters would be an exciting and welcome addition to your Little University experience, here are some tips to get started:

1. Select a date that works for you.

   - Each library system has a different requirement for how far in advance a program needs to be booked in order to be added to promotional materials in time for printing. However, fire stations may not know their schedules that far in advance and may not be able to confirm until a month before the program or later. In our experience, fire stations are nearly always available for programs when booked in advance, but you can call your station to verify if you have not heard from them and are concerned.

   - Fire station websites (especially those in larger cities) usually have a page where community members can request a fire truck and firefighters for community events. Fill out this page with as much information as you can (including the date and time of your program, your address, and what the program will look like) and save a copy of the submission. Follow up with the fire station if you have not received confirmation by the date outlined on their intake form.

2. Ensure that you follow the guidelines of your organization (if any).

- Some organizations require that all outside presenters submit to a background check or other formality before being scheduled. Check with your supervisor or other guiding force in your library to ensure that you have followed all of these rules before moving ahead with the program. Communicate any needs that you may have to the fire department directly.

3. Have a plan.

- Fire truck storytimes can be really fun, and there are a plethora of songs and books in the world that can help make a fire truck–centered event even more exciting. If you pull together these types of materials, chances are good that they will be circulated by eager families following the end of the program.

- Some businesses sell inexpensive fire truck hats and badges that can be purchased to have on hand for the event. Alternatively, participants can create their own gear as a craft program either leading up to or during the program. Some fire stations even have hats and badges that they can bring for the children upon request.

- Should everything go according to plan and the firefighters arrive at the time the program is set to begin, invite one or more of the firefighters to participate in the stories and songs with you. They may need a bit of coaching as far as how to make sure that all of the children can see the pages of the book, how to read with inflection, and so on. But even if they are not storytime pros, the children will still be in awe!

- It is also really fun and informative for the firefighters to talk about their uniforms, what a day in the life of a firefighter is like, and about fire safety. Getting children down on the floor and crawling under "smoke" is not only educational and can save lives, but it is also really fun when the firefighters are crawling around with them.

- After talking with the firefighters, reading a story or two, and singing some songs, the highlight of the event is usually when the children get to tour the fire truck. Having nice weather for this event is ideal so that families can admire the truck from the outside as well. Depending on the climate in your area, spring and fall may be the ideal times to host such an event.

- Firefighters will often want to take photos or videos for their own purposes or to tease whatever rookie has taken the floor to present with you. If your library has specific rules about photographs and privacy, make sure to mention this to the firefighters in advance of the program.

- Thank the firefighters for their time, especially those who have actively participated in the program with you. Thank the families for coming, as well. If you are able to take pictures, doing so can add to any regular newsletter your library creates or be an excellent post on social media to garner interest in this and upcoming programs.

4. Have a backup plan.

- All fire stations will have a disclaimer even after they agree to come to the event that, should an emergency arise, the emergency takes first priority, and they will likely not be able to notify the library in this case. This means that you may end up having to do the program all by yourself and make the hats and badges even more exciting since the fire truck will be conspicuously absent.

- Look up fire safety information for children and plan an activity around it, like crawling under smoke, testing the doorknob, or dialing 911. Even if it is more exciting for a firefighter to teach you himself or herself, the Internet and your local fire station have some really great information that can be easily modified into a program activity.

- Plan on reading the books and singing the songs yourself. If it makes you more comfortable, you can set up the event like a regular weekly storytime with some familiar songs to get you from one component to the next.

- Invite pretend play so that the children in attendance can imagine being firefighters themselves. Even having some sort of honorary firefighter certification would be fun and would be something the children could happily take home with them.

5. Promote the program, carefully.

    •   Because the firefighters may be called away at the last minute and may not show up at all, it is important to inform families of this unfortunate possibility. Instead of guaranteeing the presence of firefighters, including a disclaimer is a good idea when promoting the event in writing. What Mary often does is pitches the program as a "Fire Truck Storytime" and does not mention firefighters at all in any print collateral. When speaking with customers in the library, however, she includes the possibility of "special guests" arriving, along with the caveat. It is then up to the parents to communicate this to their children or not and, if so, how to go about doing that. Encouraging children to wear costumes can also be a way to make the program exciting even if the firefighters are unable to attend.

6. Cross your fingers!

    •   After confirming with your library and the fire station and everything is out in the world, cross your fingers that the firefighters will arrive. If they are not there right at the beginning of the program, start as though they will not be there at all and be flexible with your programming if they happen to roll in part way through.

    •   It is important to communicate your desires to the other staff members in the building so that they can talk to the firefighters if you are in the middle of the program when they arrive. This not only helps things go more smoothly for you, but it gets your library staff on board with the program, as well.

Police Officers

Especially in today's precarious political climate, police officers can have as much a negative stigma as firefighters have a positive one. That is all the more reason to invite them in for a story or two to show the children (*and* the parents) that what they may have seen in the media does not represent every officer.

1. Make contact.

    •   The community resource officer is the person most likely to be interested in and available for the program itself. Determine what district your library is a part of and contact the district to learn who the community resource officer is. Sometimes, this person will also attend local neighborhood meetings and you can make contact with them directly at these kinds of events. Either way, you will want their name and information, and you will want to make sure they have yours.

2. Meet any additional requirements of your library system.

    •   As mentioned earlier, if your library requires that outside present- ers of all kinds follow any sort of protocol, ensure that you have met all of these requirements.

3. Plan the program.

    •   When the community resource officer agrees to do the program, find a date that works for both of you within the guidelines of your mutual organizations. Depending on the community resource offi- cer, he or she may have limited availability, which may affect the date or time of your program. He or she may also wish to know what your plan for the event might be ahead of time so he or she can adequately prepare. Keep lines of communication strong to ensure comfort on both sides.

    •   Find books and songs that have to do with police officers and are age appropriate for your community. Community resource offi- cers also often have badge stickers that they will bring for the chil- dren, so ask about that if you have not been told already.

    •   If there are no stickers available, make a police badge as a craft leading up to or following the program.

    •   Encourage the community resource officer to bring information and to talk about their job. If you know what they will talk about, you can help design activities based on the lessons he or she wishes to teach. If you do not, remain flexible and enhance any new information with tie-ins from your own experiences with your families.

4. Promote the program.

    •   Use your library's print and digital resources to promote the pro- gram far and wide. Like firefighters, there is a chance that the community resource officer may be called away at the last minute or may have to leave early, so use your judgment as far as whether you include their presence in your promotion of the program. Plan to do the program with or without the community resource officer there, and make sure to communicate with your staff the possibilities of what could happen on that day. Encourage costumes for more fun.

5. Do the program.

   • Like the program with the firefighters, plan to be doing the program by yourself, but be flexible if/when the community resource officer arrives. Though you will be taking the lead, allow the community resource officer to read stories and sing songs as he or she is comfortable throughout the duration of the program.

6. Follow up with customers after the program.

   • This may be more important for the adults than for the children, as some may be less comfortable with the presence of a police officer than others. If you notice that someone is uncomfortable, find a moment to speak privately with them and introduce them directly to the community resource officer if they are willing. Getting feedback after this program, either positive or negative, can help dictate whether having a regular program with a community resource officer might be beneficial to the community or not.

Doctors

Doctors can be some of the most accessible outside presenters the library can have. This is particularly because they can come on their own schedule and are likely already a library user themselves. As you get to know the community in which you work by talking to library users at the desk and in and around storytimes, you are likely to find someone who is a doctor or a nurse themselves and may be more than willing to come in and present with you.

1. Identify at least one (possibly more than one) option.

   • Talk to your storytime families. Talk to your staff. Talk to the people who come to the desk to ask about or circulate materials. As you get to know the people who frequent your library, you will begin to build rapport with them and that rapport will lead to possible collaborations. Make note of medical professionals that you come across and tell them about your program and its goals. If they are interested in participating, invite them to do so. If there are more than one, see if they might want to participate together, especially if they have different medical specialties.

- If you are unable to identify someone using this method, reach out to your local doctor's offices and hospitals to see if they do community outreach or have someone who might be willing to come talk to your children and families.

2. Discuss the program and its goals and find a date that works.

- The more the merrier for this kind of program, for kids and adults alike. If you have a few people who are interested, tell them about Little University and the goals you have for the program. They may have ideas that you had not considered and may be willing to collaborate on something more than you had imagined. Find a date that works for everyone within the confines of your organization and your program.
- If your library has specific requirements for outside presenters, make sure that they are met before moving forward.

3. Plan the program.

- Use the talents of the people with whom you are working to make the program a success. This can mean educating children about the way a stethoscope works, bringing in stuffed animals for "medical treatment" in the form of bandages or thermometers, and more. The medical professionals with whom you are collaborating may have access to kid-friendly equipment to use, or you may be able to find donations or items you can borrow from a local hospital or doctor's office.
- Pick out some books and songs to break up the talking and activity.
- Print song sheets for everyone, and get together to practice ahead of time if that makes sense for all of your presenters.

4. Promote the program.

- Use the print and digital collateral at your library to promote the program, and promote within the library through word of mouth. Encourage your participants to share the event with their colleagues and patients as makes sense.
- These presenters will most likely be able to do the program and will not be called away at the last minute. However, it is still a good idea to have a contingency plan, just in case.

5. Provide further activities or information for families after the program.

    *   As this program may be more interactive than other programs with community helpers, providing more information and activities for families to take home can make a big difference. Whether that is information on local first-aid classes or places to receive income-based medical care (or something else) is up to you. Often, people will have questions that they are unwilling to ask in the moment, so if the medical professionals are willing to share their information, providing that to the families can be equally helpful.

Garbage Truck Drivers

Garbage trucks hold perhaps the highest esteem behind emergency vehicles in the eyes of young children. One of Mary's regular storytime participants came dressed as a garbage truck for Halloween, and she went home and told her husband about the adorable encounter. He then said, "why don't you do a garbage truck storytime?" Mary thought about regular storytime and wondered if there would be enough material for one devoted specifically to garbage trucks, but then her husband clarified: "Why don't you do one with an *actual* garbage truck?" And thus, the idea was born.

1. Reach out.

    *   Mary had no idea whether or not Denver Public Works would be willing or able to provide a program for the library, so she found their contact information and asked them. The City's Public Works website usually has contact information listed, so take a moment to reach out to them, explain the program, and what you would specifically like from the Public Works department. Give them a few days to respond.

    *   If they are interested, as was the case for Mary, they will respond and may ask for more information. In that case, continue a dialogue with them to determine what makes sense for everyone.

    *   If your library has specific requirements for outside presenters, ensure that those are met before continuing with this process.

2. Schedule the program.

    *   If everyone is on board, use the guidelines of your library and the Public Works Department to select a date that is mutually beneficial and confirm it.

- In Mary's case, the Public Works staff usually do not work on Saturdays, the day when her Little University programs occur. However, they were so enthusiastic about participating in the program that they were able to work with their supervisors in order to make it happen.

- Unfortunately, after this program took place, Public Works determined that it was no longer within its scope to provide this kind of community outreach. It definitely does not hurt to reach out to your community, but please be aware that it is always a possibility that agencies may not be able to participate for reasons beyond your (or their) control.

3. Plan the program.

- Select stories and songs about garbage trucks to incorporate into a storytime-esque setting. Invite the Public Works employees to talk about their jobs, explain their uniform, and share other interesting facts and anecdotes about the job.

- Some excellent additional information to include could be the color of the garbage truck (if there are different colors for different purposes), the parts of a garbage truck and what they do, and the uniform pieces that garbage truck drivers are required to wear and why.

- Prepare an activity for the participants to do either during or after the program, perhaps scattering "trash" in the form of paper scraps around the floor and having them pick up that trash. However, if the Public Works team is able to bring a real garbage truck along with them, this activity may or may not be necessary.

4. Promote the program.

- Use the print and digital collateral available to you through your library to promote the program. Public Works is much less likely to be called away to an emergency than firefighters or police might be, so promoting them in the print collateral is likely safe. Talk about the program with your colleagues and in storytimes to build the momentum, interest, and awareness necessary to make it successful. Encourage costumes related to the program for even more fun.

5. Do the program.

- Have everything ready and prepared for Public Works staff to be able to step in and comfortably participate in the program. Ensure that there is enough space for the activities you have prepared and that song sheets or other needs are in place before the event begins.

- Talk with the Public Works team who will be presenting with you ahead of time to make sure that they are comfortable with the format and to see if they have other ideas for how the event can go. You can also provide books to them so that they can select the one or ones they are most comfortable presenting. Fiction and nonfiction are excellent options in this case.

- Weather permitting, invite customers out to the garbage truck for a demonstration of how it functions, if possible.

- Take pictures if it is allowed by your library to share with others how the program went. Have books and other materials available for people to check out and take home with them to talk even more about garbage trucks after the event. Though there are fewer unknowns with this presentation than with presentations from other public servants, be prepared to go with the flow. If the presenter is not comfortable or familiar with talking to children and families, you may have to "translate" for them. If you get a larger audience than you expect, help safely transition families from one location to the next.

- Most importantly, thank the Public Works team for taking the time to present this program. Parents may have more questions than the children with regard to trash pickup or other needs, so be aware of these conversations and feel free to help extract the presenters if necessary.

Local Businesses and Destination Storytimes

Depending on the neighborhood, local businesses may be an excellent way to mutually benefit both the library and the business *and* provide an early literacy experience outside the traditional library setting. In the case of libraries in which there is no separate meeting room for storytime like Mary's, programs with local businesses can be a way to be rowdy or to offer a different experience without having to work around the limitations of a small library setting. By working in tandem with a local business, both parties can promote the program to their regular customers, thus cross-pollinating and bringing those who frequent the library and those who frequent the business together under one roof. Following the program, the library may get more users and the business may get more customers, and all will remember the positive experience that introduced them to these new settings.

1. Evaluate your neighborhood and target potential options.

    •   Every neighborhood is different and has its own unique style. Some neighborhoods have a pub or local eatery that functions as its center point. Others have an ice-cream shop or café. You know your neighborhood best, so you are best suited to determine what those hot spots might be. If you are not sure, talk with your customers to see where they like to go nearby. Build relationships with them and see if there might be some hidden gems that would be perfect but that you might not have otherwise noticed.

    •   Good options include:

        ○   Places that cater to children often, like ice-cream shops or toy stores.

        ○   Places the family enjoys frequenting together, like local breweries, bakeries, or coffee shops.

        ○   Local businesses that want to become more visible and increase their footprint in the neighborhood.

        ○   Places with large floor space for seating for a storytime event.

2. Reach out.

    •   Once you have narrowed down your options, reach out to each business. Set up an appointment to speak with the owner about the project, the library, and how participating in a program together would be mutually beneficial.

3. Determine cost or if the program will be done for free.

    •   Some companies are happy to provide the program free of charge, as they are earning potential new paying customers through the arrangement.

    •   Others may require some sort of honorarium in order to keep afloat.

    •   Decide what works best for both of you, considering the amount of effort that each party is contributing to the event itself.

4. Ask about any freebies for participants.

    •   Nearly anywhere you might consider doing an outreach storytime event is likely to have food or beverage as its center point. If you are doing an event at an ice-cream shop, see about the possibility of providing ice cream for all participants. If you are going to a coffee shop, perhaps cake or pastries might be more logical. When there is the draw of free food or goodies, people are more inclined to attend the program and leave happy.

- If there is a need for an honorarium, it may be to cover the cost of these goodies.

5. Follow up with any requirements of the library system.

- If your library system requires background checks or anything else from outside presenters, make sure to follow those guidelines and rules before finalizing any program.

6. Schedule the program.

- Find a time that is mutually beneficial to host the program. Usually, this will take place outside of normal business hours for the business itself in order to ensure that there is space and focus for the program. This may also mean that it will take place outside of normal Little University programming time. Adjust library staff schedules accordingly if these events fall outside of normal operating hours for the library.

7. Promote the program.

- Use print and digital collateral to promote the program within the library. If possible, share the event on social media with the business with which you will be working so that they can share it with their customers, as well. Bring print material to the business for staff to hand out to people who frequent the store. Talk about the program with library customers during and outside of storytime. If there is a limit to the number of people who can attend, make sure to note that. If you are meeting specifically at the business, make sure to note that, too. Encourage appropriate outfits if the occasion calls for it (PJ Storytime, Halloween events, etc.)

8. Execute the program.

- Work closely with the business to meet ahead of time to explain in detail how the program will go. Mary prepares the storytime using songs that are appropriate to the occasion, makes song sheets, and selects books. Making all of these available to the business ahead of time helps their employees participate more fully in the program and feel more comfortable doing so.

- Depending on the business, you may have people willing to play the ukulele but not read aloud, or the business may already have a program for children and you can work together to create something that blends the two approaches.

- However it works for everyone to be comfortable will be the most successful.

- If you have goodies in the form of food or something else, wait until the end of the program to pass them out so that people are focused on the program while it is taking place.

- If you have a limited number of goodies, prepare a card or popsicle stick with numbers ahead of time. Pass these out as people arrive to help keep track of how many are in attendance and to ease the queuing process for treats at the end.

9. Evaluate the program and determine if it will be done again.

- Thank the business representatives immediately after the program and help clean up.

- Thank the business representatives again in an e-mail for working with you.

- Discuss with your colleagues whether the attendance, work involved, and outcome warrants considering repeating the program at another point.

- Bear in mind that, often, the success of these programs comes from their novelty. If you have one successful program at an ice-cream shop, for example, and schedule another one a couple of months later, the second may not be as successful as the first. Perhaps it works best for your library to have a program at this business once a year, or perhaps more, or less, often. Each situation is different, as is the work that goes into it.

- If you can, track the time and effort each program took along with any costs associated and overall feedback and outcome. These measurements can help determine the benefit of repeating the event or if anything needs to be adjusted before it can be attempted again.

- Each event gets easier—it can be intimidating to do a storytime with people who may not do storytime regularly outside your familiar storytime space and possibly at a different time, but doing so provides families with fun, safe, unique activities to do together, and the benefits are often immeasurable.

VIP Community Member Storytimes

This program idea is meant to build off those already listed in this section. Children and families interact with their communities in many different ways on a daily basis. Think of what community members your families might be touched to find providing an early learning program for them. This may be your mayor or district City Council person, or simply the supervisor of your library. If your library location has a security guard, this individual is a great choice to welcome into your program series, as sometimes a uniform is intimidating or off-putting to children (and adults). You might even invite the director of a nearby preschool or a kindergarten teacher to facilitate this program with you.

As mentioned earlier, you will likely do most of the prep work for your VIP community member. Their job will be to arrive, interact with the families present, and look silly participating in songs and dances. That said, hopefully your community member will also appreciate the chance to read a story aloud to your families.

We suggest including the book *Clothesline Clues to Jobs People Do* (Kathryn Heling) in your program's introduction. This will orient your participants to different jobs people are doing in their community and be an excellent segue to introducing your guest of honor.

If your guest has an activity of interest or expertise, wrap up your program by providing the supplies for them to lead your families in this activity. Perhaps your mayor does origami, or your library supervisor paints watercolors. Or, if you have invited someone from a preschool or kindergarten, perhaps he or she can provide an example activity of what children will experience on their first day of school. This may be as simple as a cup of Play-Doh or a worksheet to color on.

Conclude your program by allowing time for your VIP community member to chat directly with families. Many caregivers may have questions for, or want a picture of their child with, your guest of honor. Others will simply appreciate getting to know someone they interact with regularly but do not usually speak with at length.

This program option is especially relevant to communities going through change, whether it is a local election or a social justice movement.

Your early learning program series can be an excellent opportunity to bring communities together and bridge otherwise growing divides.

STEM Programs

As mentioned in the previous chapter, STEM (science, technology, engineering, and math) programs are often intimidating to people who do not venture into this realm very often. However, there are many ways to incorporate these ideas into programs in your library in ways that are fun for both program leaders and program participants.

Donated-Supply Planting Projects

This is a wonderful program due to its take-home component, where children will continue to care for seeds and seedlings until they grow into plants. It is also a beautiful way to involve your entire community in one of your early learning programs, as you will ideally solicit donations for this program from your library users!

Materials

- Planting containers: egg cartons and berry containers work best. Left-over seedling starting containers are obviously going to work well, and many members of your community (including yourself!) may have these on hand from starting their own gardens. You could also contact your local gardening store for these containers or broken pots they can no longer sell (simply sand down rough edges ahead of time).
- Seeds or starter plants: seeds are the easiest way to go here. Ask community members to bring you seeds from their seed packets for easy-to-grow plants like radishes, green beans, snap or snow peas, and basil. All of these seeds require little effort and will sprout in a short period of time.
- Soil: again, ask your community members to save a bit from bags of potting soil and bring that in to you. You will not need very much! Alternately, ask your local gardening store to donate some to you.
- Table covers: old newspapers will be just fine for this!
- Potted plants or pictures of plants to use as examples.
- For fun, you could provide actual examples of whatever you are planting like radishes, snow peas, or even fresh basil leaves, for participants

to taste. (You may even be able to get these small quantities donated from your nearby grocery store!)

Process

1. Begin your program by introducing the plants, either via real plants or via pictures of plants. Then, pass out your little samples of what each plant's fruit or leaves taste like. While everyone is munching (or spitting out!), demonstrate how the program will go.

2. Participants will begin by scooping potting soil into their planting containers, using their hands to do so. Exploring different textures is a great way to stimulate sensory learning!

3. Then, each participant will create a tiny hole in the top of their planter in which they should place their seeds. Participants should be given three of the same seed to ensure that at least one will sprout. Hopefully, you have had enough supplies donated so that your participants can plant multiple kinds of plants!

4. After placing the seeds, children should carefully cover them with a bit more potting soil, and then take them home to water and care for until the plants are sprouted!

5. You can suggest that families take a digital picture of the plant at the same time every day to watch it grow and change since this growth happens too slowly for us to observe directly.

DIY Play-Doh

This program has mutual benefits for participants, including the science of how each element goes together and getting to play with the dough afterward. Getting a fun toy to take home and play with again and again is exciting by itself, and the fact that doing so increases hand strength is an added bonus.

There are two ways to make Play-Doh: one involves heating the dough and one does not. Depending on the materials available to you, you may choose one or the other as a more accessible option. Both are educational and easy to execute. Though these materials are relatively inexpensive, if your budget is extremely small, they are often materials that can be procured from other library users or staff as donations if necessary.

Materials

To make Play-Doh by cooking *you will need:*

- One cup of plain, all-purpose flour
- One cup of water
- Two teaspoons of cream of tartar
- One-third cup of salt
- One tablespoon of vegetable oil
- Food coloring (optional, but a great learning tool)
- Heating element (portable is ideal, especially if you can get it close to ground level so children can see inside of it. Something deep enough for the Play-Doh but shallow enough to see into.)
- Heat-safe mixing spoon
- Tall, clear container for visibly mixing liquids
- Plastic zipper bags or portion cups with lids to take the Play-Doh home

To make Play-Doh without cooking *you will need:*

- Two cups of plain, all-purpose flour
- Two tablespoons of vegetable oil
- A half cup of salt
- Two tablespoons of cream of tartar
- Up to 1.5 cups of boiling water (adding in increments until reaching the right consistency)
- Food coloring (optional, but a great learning tool)
- Large bowl
- Mixing spoon
- Tall, clear container for visibly mixing liquids
- Plastic zipper bags or portion cups with lids to take the Play-Doh home

Process

We recommend trying at least one option before the program starts to ease your comfort with it and to determine if you need to increase the portion size for the number of participants you anticipate having. Whatever recipe you decide to use, having printed versions available for families to take home and replicate is a must!

Instructions: (Both processes start out the same way and only diverge when it comes to the heating portion as will be described here).

1. Make sure all of your ingredients and supplies are in place before the program begins and are visible to your audience. If you have access to a lab coat, that would be an excellent, although not mandatory, addition.

2. Welcome everyone to the program and talk a little bit about the science of cooking, as that is more or less what will be taking place. You can discuss this in as much specificity as you are comfortable doing. Something as simple as "we are going to be turning all of these ingredients into something else," works just as well as a more-complex explanation.

3. Start by mixing your wet ingredients in the tall, clear plastic container. No matter which recipe you are using, do not use all of the water here; a partial amount is sufficient. The purpose of mixing these in the large, clear container is to explain a bit about density and how water and oil do not mix.

    a. First, put in some of the water (again, not all of the water you will need for your recipe).

    b. Next, you will add your oil. But before you do, ask your audience what they think will happen. Will it dissolve into the water? Or will something else happen? Then, pour it in and discuss the results of your "experiment."

    c. Next, you will be adding food coloring. If you are comfortable soliciting opinions as to what color to use, feel free to do so. If not, just use one color that you will have determined before the start of the program. Like with the oil, ask your participants what they think will happen when the food coloring is put into the mixture. Using words like "experiment" and "I wonder" are ways to encourage the scientific process without giving the impression that there is one right answer.

    d. If all has worked in this process, the oil will sit on top of the water (let it settle before adding the food coloring) and the food coloring will remain in drops through the oil before dispersing into the water below. Expect some "oohs" and "aahs" here!

e. Now that the liquids are together, set them aside to work with the dry ingredients. As you add them to the bowl or portable heating element (depending on which method you are using), explain what you are doing and invite everyone to count with you as you add different numbers of things (there is some math to go with the science!)

f. Now, you can add the liquids to the dry ingredients, once again asking the participants what they think will happen. Remember to add in any more water called for by the recipe you are using. In both cases, heat will play a part in the mixing process, although it will be more readily visible inside the portable heating element. Talk about what you see happening as you begin mixing all of the ingredients together. Is there anything surprising happening?

g. Mix the ingredients until you reach the desired consistency. It should be soft and malleable but not sticky. If it gets too dry, add more water. If it is too sticky, cook it longer or add more flour (depending on your method).

h. Once the Play-Doh is complete, portion it out to each child. If you have cooked the Play-Doh, make sure you encourage the parents to test the end result first to prevent any burns or injuries. If you are using boiling water, you will also want to check this, although it is likely to cool more quickly.

i. Depending on your setup, you may have table space for everyone or you may have plastic trays laid out on the floor. No matter what the setup, now is the time to play. Encourage discussion about what the Play-Doh feels like, smells like, and looks like. Though it is not encouraged, these recipes are safe if accidentally eaten (although they will not taste good!). If you have access to Play-Doh plastic tools or cookie cutters, encourage experimentation with these as people are exploring. All of the squeezing required to get the dough into any shape builds hand strength that will be necessary for writing. Throw this early learning tip into the mix as people are playing!

j. Both recipes will stay usable for at least a couple of months if treated properly. Give everyone a baggie or portion cup in which to store their dough and remind them that if it goes a little dry, they can always add a touch of water to enliven it again.

Clay and Bead Gardens

This program is a wonderful way to build off of the previous program, or can be accomplished with donated or cheaply purchased supplies. It is one of the simplest programs we have offered, but has families asking for it over and over. If your group is up for it, introduce this program by reading *The Lorax* (Dr. Seuss) aloud.

Materials

- Clay: absolutely any kind will do. Play-Doh works, actual clay that a potter or ceramics studio might donate, works. Store-bought clay works. Whatever you can get your hands on. Participants will need only enough to form one hand-sized disc, though more is welcome.
- Pipe cleaners; aka chenille sticks.
- Pony beads: you can also provide large buttons (buttons with holes big enough to thread a chenille stick through).

Process

1. Begin either by reading together or by jumping straight into the demonstration of how the project works.
2. Participants will first thread beads and buttons (either closely together or spaced apart—it does not matter!) onto chenille sticks. Parents with babies can either do this themselves or skip the beads entirely. About four or five bead-covered chenille sticks per participant will be perfect.
3. Then, participants will twist the chenille sticks around their fingers to form curls or loops or whatever. The more whimsical, the better.
4. From here, participants will grab a hunk of clay and form it into a disc about the size of their hand.
5. Participants will then "plant" their chenille sticks into the clay disc. They may stand straight up, bend over, or be attached to the clay on both ends. Looping the chenille sticks around or through each other makes for a beautiful finished product.
6. Ideally, you have enough supplies for each family to make another clay garden as children learn through repetition and love to repeat a process they have just mastered! Either way, allow the clay gardens to go home to window sills or bedside tables where they will dry into whimsical little gardens.

Found Object Robots

We like to call this program "Tinker Time," since participants are basically using found objects to create *whatever* they want. Giving the outcome the name "Robot," though, helps parents visualize an end goal.

Materials

- Cardboard cartons: milk cartons, rinsed out, are ideal. In a pinch, tissue boxes or cracker/snack boxes will also work. Give everything a quick rinse or wipe down before offering it to your group. Every child will need one of these items as the base of their project.
- Wood glue, Mod Podge, and/or glue guns. Adults will be managing this component of the project, but be extra cautious if glue guns are around, for obvious reasons.
- Duct tape, especially in cool colors. Painter's tape and/or electrical tape will also work.
- Scissors for cutting the tape.
- Piles of found objects: bottle caps, soda bottle tops, and jar lids all make great robot eyes, ears, and buttons. Chenille sticks, actual sticks from outside, pieces of dowel rods, and popsicle sticks make good antennae and arms. Toilet paper tubes or paper towel tubes cut into about one-inch cylinders make nice, sturdy robot legs. Yarn or string makes fun robot hair.
- Paint and paintbrushes, if you want.
- Wide-tipped permanent markers, if you are daring.

Process

1. You might begin your program by singing "Head, Shoulders, Knees and Toes" and talking about our body parts: torso, head, arms, hair, ears, eyes, and legs, specifically.
2. Then, show participants an example robot you have made in advance, or simply walk through the supplies with them, allowing them to suggest what you might use each different object to represent (i.e., would this bottle cap work for an arm? Not really, but maybe for an eyeball or a shirt button!).
3. Give your caregivers a quick tour of your fastening options: the glue, hot glue, and tape selection. That will be their primary duty throughout this program.

4. Children will then be given the "body" of their robot (one of the car-
    tons or boxes) and sent to the supplies to begin their project. Remind
    parents that, as always, this is about process over product: thinking
    about our bodies and body parts and then using fine motor skills to
    replicate these body parts on a robot.

5. If you want, you can allow participants to paint their robots or color in
    their robots with permanent markers. We tend to provide the markers,
    or nothing, since the texture of the cartons/ boxes makes paint about
    the least likely thing to stick to them. Families tend to be maxed out
    once the robots are assembled anyway and are not likely to want to
    continue with decorating them. Still, you could have paint or markers
    on hand in case you are asked about this finishing touch!

Wellness Programs

Children who are chronically stressed have an extremely difficult time
learning. While an early learning program series obviously cannot eliminate stressors children may be facing, some early learning programs can
provide tools for children to use to manage that stress.

Glittery Calming Jars

Calming jars work like timers but are prettier to look at and more men-
tally stimulating to watch. Providing a child with a calming jar to take
home can help caregivers manage time-outs or redirect overly energetic
behaviors. Additionally, children may find their calming jars soothing to
watch at naptime or bedtime.

Materials

*   Pint-sized mason jars, spaghetti sauce jars, or pickle jars with labels
    removed. In a pinch, plastic water bottles with labels removed will work.
*   Super glue or a hot glue gun. You will be the only person working with
    this material, so whatever you are most comfortable with will work.
*   Pitchers of *warm* water or, even better, a sink.
*   Clear dishwashing liquid soap; just a little.
*   Glitter glue, enough for each child to have about two ounces. One standard-
    sized bottle is about six ounces; given that little hands are using this
    material, we would plan for one bottle for every two participants.

- Glitter to match the color(s) of the glitter glue. You will need a *lot*, maybe up to one entire jar per participant. It is a good idea to check with your facilities team regarding the glitter. To save them a headache, consider moving the program outside or placing plastic on the floor to ease cleanup. Glitter has a way of traveling and multiplying!
- Food coloring to match the color(s) of the glitter glue and glitter.
- Ideally, a helper for you!

Process

1. This program works best when taking each step all together as a group, since many of the materials can be spilled easily and in some cases may require semi-precise measurements. Regardless, begin the program by showing an example calming jar you have already made yourself. Pass it around and allow children to explore turning it right-side up, upside down, and sideways to watch the glitter float around.

2. Provide each child with a jar of their own, and ask them all to remove the lid. Caregivers with babies will do the entire process for their babies and then allow babies to watch the jars work.

    a. Begin by pouring warm water and glitter glue into the jar together. You will want the jar about ¾ full of warm water, then add the glitter glue. Participants will then put the lid tightly onto the jar, and shake until the glue has dissolved into warm water. Your helper will assist caregivers in making sure the lids are tight before the shaking begins. The color of the glitter glue is the color the calming jar will turn out to be. Therefore, either have participants select their color in advance, or provide all the same color. Blue is a very peaceful color for a calming jar.

    b. Reopen the jar and dump in the glitter. This is the most fun part for the children, though obviously a glitter spill is not an ideal outcome. Perhaps prep this step by having children pretend to sprinkle, dust, and pour slowly before providing the actual glitter. Remember to use whatever color of glitter matches the glitter glue color!

    c. Have your helper assist you in providing the food coloring. Children will only need two to three drops of food coloring; too much will result in the glitter being obscured by a dark color. Caregivers might prefer to do this for children, or you might prefer to do it yourself. Again, remember to use the same color food coloring as glitter glue and glitter. Mixing colors will make the jar look muddy.

d. Screw the lid on once more, and give the jar a test. The contents should swirl like a snow globe and take about 30 to 60 seconds to settle. If any contents are looking too thin or watery, add the clear dishwashing liquid until the settling process reaches the desired timeline. The more dishwashing liquid, the slower the settling process.

e. Once this step is completed, families should carefully bring their jars to you for the final step. You will squirt super glue or hot glue around the rim of the jar and then screw the lid on. This final step gives parents peace of mind about taking these jars home!

3. It is nice to conclude this program all together, as it began, but this time with each child having their own jar to swirl and watch. You could even dim the lights and take a few deep breaths together, since the process of making the jars with so many spillable ingredients is likely to raise some anxiety levels in the room!

Smoothie Samplers

Healthy eating is key to early learning success, and a program that uses a blender and fruit is sure to be a hit with little ones you are encouraging toward healthy eating! The goal here is not to convert your families to smoothie making, but rather to simply expose them to different options for getting key nutrients into their children. Possibilities here are endless, and you can take this program in as many directions as smoothie recipes you can find online. Here is one option that worked well for us!

Materials

- Two or more blenders, plus extension cords to avoid any tripping. Providing one blender per table is ideal! For extra safety, tape the cords to the floor or cover with a rug to prevent tripping.

- Measuring cups. A one-cup measuring cup per table is ideal. This is a very, *very* simple smoothie formula.

- Small cups. You could use clear plastic punch cups or even the small paper cups many folks keep near the bathroom sink. You will be making more than one kind of smoothie, we hope, so each participant will need only a small amount of each one.

- Smoothie ingredients:

    - Liquid: almond milk or coconut milk. Avoid dairy due to possible allergies. You will need one to two cups per blender.

    - Soft fruit: banana. You could do avocado, but the process of cutting open an avocado may be a bit much. You will want one to two bananas per blender. (You can also provide bags of frozen bananas, now available at some grocery stores!)

    - Frozen fruit: peaches and berries are classic choices. Pineapple is another great option. You will want one to two adult handfuls per blender.

    - Greens: have fun with this, since once the greens are blended in, children will not be able to taste them! Spinach is a classic, but kale is another great option. One large bag of greens should cover your entire program, as each blender will only need about a cup.

    - Flavor enhancers, *if* you want. Honey is a classic, but is not recommended for babies. Agave nectar is a nice sweetener that would work instead. You could also provide cinnamon, cocoa powder, or vanilla extract. You will only need between one teaspoon and one tablespoon each, if any.

    - Ice cubes.

    - Extra fruit and greens to use while introducing your program.

Process

Families will work together in small groups for this program, but everyone will begin all together with you. You will introduce the concept of the program by providing tiny bites of fruit and one or two green leaves for each child to try. You can talk about how they taste and whether kids like them or not. Caregivers should join in this taste test, feeling free to admit that sometimes, they too do not care for raw greens! Let everyone know that you all will be working to create different smoothie concoctions and then will all have the chance to sample each one that is prepared!

1. As with the previous program, this program works best when taken one step at a time with the whole group. Begin with each table selecting what milk they would like to try, and then adding one cup of that milk to their blender. We listed almond and coconut above, but many

nondairy milks are available and you may find yourself with a wider variety of options.

2. From here, add one banana or a cup of frozen banana pieces to the blender. Pop the lid on and allow each child a chance to pulse or blend this mixture for a few seconds. If you are using fresh bananas and want to add ice to the mixture (so that it is cold), now is the time to do so! Just about a half cup of ice will do.

3. Take the lid off and add the frozen fruit. Any mixture works, and this is the time for children to get creative! Strawberries are a classic, but strawberries and pineapple mixed together is especially yummy. Peach and blueberry is another great combination. (If you have had loads of time to prepare, perhaps you can consider freezing fruit for the program yourself. Watermelon is a particularly interesting option to provide!) You will need about one to two adult handfuls, or cups, of frozen fruit, total. Have the children take turns pulsing or blending for another few seconds once the fruit is added in.

4. Then, toss in a handful of greens. Give the smoothie another few pulses or another 30 seconds or so of blending, until it is smooth. Be aware that over-blending will result in a warm (but still drinkable) smoothie, so encourage self-control with this step.

5. Now comes the fun part! Provide a cup to each child, and have them sample the smoothie they have just made. We hope they love it! Then encourage each family to sample the smoothies made by other families in this program. If you were able to provide multiple blenders, hopefully your families will have four to five smoothies to taste test!

Nut-Free Trail Mix Tastings

Building off of the preceding program, but without any appliances, we suggest providing an option for families to learn a quick recipe or two for healthy, inexpensive snacks they can take on the go. For caregivers with babies, encourage them to make these snacks for themselves, as self-care is incredibly important for parents—especially new ones!

Materials

- Measuring cups: One set per table would be ideal, but really anything will work. As earlier, we will try to provide measurements in "handfuls" as well as in precise amounts.

- Bowls: You might provide one large bowl per table, or individual bowls for each family to use. We like encouraging families to work together as groups by providing one large bowl, as this is especially inclusive for caregivers who are not familiar with the program concept or are not comfortable with English instructions.

- Zipper seal plastic baggies, ideally enough for each participant to take home a sampling of each trail mix made. For a program with about 20 families, one box of these bags should cover it!

- Ingredients:

  - Seeds: we suggest pumpkin seeds and sunflower seeds. You can also provide flax or hemp seeds, if you want to be extra creative.

  - Something salty: we like pretzel sticks or Goldfish crackers. Store-bought popcorn is a great, unexpected addition.

  - Sweet chips: you could do milk chocolate chips, dark chocolate chips, cacao nibs, butterscotch chips, yogurt covered raisins, M&Ms, or all of the above!

  - Dried fruit: we think raisins and dried coconut flakes are essential. Dried dates, cranberries, blueberries, apricots, and cherries are also great options. (You may have to cut the dried apricots into smaller pieces.)

  - Dehydrated fruit: bananas are essential here. Dehydrated mango pieces and apple slices are also great options.

Display your ingredients. We like to leave everything in the bags in which they were purchased so that caregivers are very clear about what each item is. If you want a more pleasing display, pour each ingredient separately into bowls with the bags nearby. Either way, have everything out together on one large table, as you will want participants to be able to pick and choose from all available options.

Process

1. Begin by creating a trail mix together as a group. This will ensure that each family has at least one "good" trail mix to try!

   a. An ideal trail mix concoction will have about two part seeds to one part everything else. So two cups of seeds, one cup of pretzel sticks, a half cup of chocolate chips, a half cup of butterscotch chips, a cup of dried cranberries, and a cup of dehydrated banana slices would be an example.

   b. You can pass this around and encourage bites of each individual ingredient. As earlier, open conversation about what is liked and disliked, and encourage caregivers to share as well!

2. Give each child a bowl or, ideally, direct families to take a place at one of your tables. From here, nearly anything goes. Roughly follow the formula above, and you will have several great snacks from which to choose.

3. Allow time for children to first try their own concoction, and then to try each other's. Using your measuring cups, portion out about a quarter cup to a half cup of the trail mixes for your families to take home. Some participants will want some of each, while others will only be interested in the one they made. Encourage parents to also select one or two to take home for themselves!

4. As a take-home add-on, you might have the ability to provide index cards or recipe cards for parents to note what their children particularly liked in order to replicate this at home!

Fruit Salads or Kabobs

Food programs may take extra prep work, but providing your families with a free, nutritious snack and a free, nutritious snack idea is worth the trouble, in our opinion. A fruit salad or kabob program gives children many opportunities to use simple kitchen tools while putting together something tasty and nutritious to eat!

Materials

- Cutting boards or sanitizer for tables.
- Butter knives or plastic knives ideally, one per child.
- Plastic cereal bowls and either spoons or bamboo kabob sticks.
- Fruit salad or kabob ingredients:
  - Soft fruit: melon (watermelon, cantaloupe, etc.), banana, ripe pear, or all of the above. Try mango if you are adventurous and have extra time to prep!

- Crunchy fruit: apples are ideal here. Go ahead and buy presliced apples to save yourself some time, if you can! You will need to go ahead and have these cut into bite-sized pieces. (Quick tip: You can use grapes here, but grapes are a common choking hazard, so we recommend cutting them in half if you decide to use them. To do this quickly, put your grapes onto a dinner plate or paper plate. Hold another plate on top firmly, face down. Slide a sharp kitchen knife through the middle of the two plates, and ta-da! Your grapes are halved!)

- Berries: strawberries, blackberries, and raspberries are great. Blueberries work well in a fruit salad, but they are a bit small for the kabobs.

- Citrus: you will only be squeezing this over the fruit, so oranges, lemons, limes, or grapefruit, cut in half, are perfect.

- Something creamy: this will be drizzled over the fruit salad like a sauce or used as a dunking option for fruit kabobs. Vanilla yogurt is a great option and is available made from nondairy milk.

- Something sprinkly: you can provide cacao nibs, shredded coconut, poppy seeds, or even colored sprinkles. You might even experiment by providing fresh mint leaves! You will only need a little, as they will lightly cover the top of the fruit salad or the top of the dunking option.

Process

1. Begin your program as above, with a bite or two of each ingredient to share around. We highly encourage this communal, group activity to start each food-based program, as eating together and talking together creates a bonding experience between child and caregiver and among your families in the program. This also ensures that any ingredients you have that may be unfamiliar to families will quickly be normalized for the purposes of your program.

2. Walk through the process of creating a fruit salad or fruit kabob together. Children will have the opportunity to slice the soft fruit themselves, so encourage them to do so! This is great for hand-eye coordination. Crunchy fruit and berries will already be the right size to add to the bowls or spear on the skewers. Demonstrate drizzling the citrus juice lightly over the fruit, and then show how the yogurt will be

used to either mix all the fruit together, or scooped into a dollop for dunking. End with a sprinkle of whatever you have to add on for the final touch!

3. From here, caregivers will work directly with children to create their fruit salad or kabob. Ideally, you will have enough ingredients for each child to create a snack for themselves and one for their caregivers. Children will enjoy this role reversal of getting to "cook" for their caregivers!

4. Allow time to enjoy eating together as a group before cleaning up your space. This will also encourage children to share what ingredients they selected for their recipes!

Language and Cultural Programs

Members of our communities come from all over the country and all over the world. Each family has unique cultural experiences that promote the melting-pot culture of our society. Getting families together to share these experiences is not only a beneficial program for your library, but it also helps bring your community closer together in understanding and acceptance. The primary desire here is to expose your Little University families to other languages and cultures, not to make them experts in anything after one session. However, having dipped their toes into this proverbial pool, more inquiry may end up taking place once the program has ended.

Language Storytimes

This type of program is likewise mentioned in the previous chapter. If you are a language savant, read on for more ideas of how to make this program work. If not, please see the previous chapter for ideas on how to get someone else to help you.

As mentioned earlier, the primary desire here is to expose children and families to other languages, not to make them fluent by the end of a 30-minute program. With the right setup and support, programs done completely in a foreign language can be understood by all even when the words themselves are unfamiliar.

Tap your librarian and family communities for people who are fluent in a language other than English. Whether it is a native fluency (i.e., they grew up speaking whatever second language it happens to be) or they studied it to the point of fluency, both are acceptable as long as they are comfortable presenting a storytime to families in that language.

Once you have found someone (or maybe more than one someone) who is willing to participate in such a program, invite them to put the program together themselves, but offer guidance if they need it. Your library may or may not have access to books in the language(s) chosen, but there are ways to make this work. By using books that may already be familiar to your participants, this adds some familiarity and comfort to the program, even when they are translated into another language.

Execution

1. Have song sheets available at the start of the program in both the target language and English to encourage participation. Goodies specific to the culture in question are also good to help segue into the experience families are about to have. If your library has materials in the language of your program, pull some together for families to examine before the event begins.

2. We highly encourage using only the target language for the duration of the program instead of attempting to use both the target language and English. While this may feel uncomfortable at first, it will encourage families to follow the cues and guidelines of the presenter instead of simply waiting for the language they understand best.

3. The presenter should include a mix of songs and books, making sure to speak clearly and enunciate while also using gestures to help communicate across the language barrier. If there are songs in English that can be easily translated into the target language (like *Head, Shoulders, Knees, and Toes*), using these will encourage participation while also teaching vocabulary. Of course, including culturally relevant songs is also helpful to promote the language and culture of the program itself.

4. An incredibly helpful component is to have you as the program lead sit among the families and encourage participation, particularly if (or when) things seem unsteady. Saying things like "you are doing a great job!" or "way to jump in on that song!" will keep families engaged and will encourage them to continue participating even if they are uncomfortable.

5. At the end of the program, thank everyone for coming both in the target language and in English, encouraging families to come talk to the presenter afterward, if desired.

Cultural Parties or Gatherings

Maybe you do not have access to someone who is comfortable conducting a full-length storytime in another language, but it is likely that you still know at least one person of another culture or background among your library staff or your community members. Put out fliers or feelers in other ways to see if there would be interest in a community cultural gathering, and then work with those people to put something together that is of interest to your library users in the context of Little University. Once again, this program is specifically designed to expose Little University participants to cultures that may be different from their own and to build a stronger sense of community among participants no matter their culture of origin.

Ideas

1. Celebrate cultural events like Dia de los Muertos, Diwali, Kwanzaa, or Chanukah on or around the dates they fall. Work with members of your community who celebrate these holidays to create events that support and encourage understanding of each celebration and what it looks like today

2. Put together a potluck (if your library permits) where people can bring flavors of their home cultures or communities together for others to try. You can play music from each represented culture to add festivity to the program.

IN SUMMARY

Despite how it may feel from time to time, you do not need to have an enormous budget in order to provide high-quality Little University programming to your community. The most important piece of this or any program is your interest in and dedication to it, as the primary benefits of the program come from those alone. Trust your instincts and your community to guide you into the most positive programming possible, using your library, early learning skills, and expertise to build and grow a program that is respected and sustainable for years to come.

YOUR TO-DO LIST

*   Determine the budget you have and how it can be used to its fullest potential.

- Investigate opportunities for ways to get materials for programs. Can you ask your community for donations? Is there a craft closet that is overflowing with odds and ends? Are there other branch locations with whom you can share?

- Compile a list of skills shared by your library staff that they would be willing to either teach you or present themselves.

- Determine what community members and icons would be available to present or co-present a program with you.

- Create a schedule with the options that are available to you, creatively utilizing the resources you already have.

FIVE

Conclusion

It is our sincere hope that this book has inspired you to establish, build upon, or improve early literacy programming within your library branch or system. Our successes came about thanks to the support of our upper management, coworkers on the ground, and above all, our communities. By sharing them with you in the pages of this book, we hope to have given you a solid foundation from which to build while being able to avoid some of the setbacks that we faced. Families across the country are actively searching for opportunities to improve their children's lives from a younger and younger age, and programs like these can make all the difference.

In a nation that is facing turbulent political times in which people are being divided more than connected, opportunities for connectedness and inclusion can be hard to find. Libraries are uniquely and ideally placed in communities nationwide as some of the only places families can gather free from bias and free of charge to learn together, build relationships, and enhance the communities in which they live. As community centers and other gathering places are disappearing, the community library must step in to fill those gaps.

As we have discussed in this book, Little University programming is designed for just this purpose. By making programming accessible to families from all cultural, linguistic, and financial backgrounds, we are providing a space for people to find equal footing. This provides equal preparation for the children in these families as they learn skills that are critical to their success in school. While storytime programs are excellent and likewise important, learning through play encourages the development of the more tactile skills that help make children successful as they grow up.

Though it might seem outside of the library's traditional scope—when people might still consider libraries to be quiet places where dusty books and dustier librarians enforce silence behind horn-rimmed glasses—we beg to differ. Gone are the days in which a library is only used as a repository for books. Today, learning happens both through reading *and* through tactile experiences. Due to the lack of other locales for this type of learning to take place in most communities, teaching skills like these is exactly within the library's scope at this point in time. Helping families to become more adept at building fine and gross motor skills, calming techniques, and critical thinking means that the children in those families will be better equipped for success in school in beyond. This, then, builds stronger and more welcoming communities moving forward.

On a much grander scale, consider this: according to the Bureau of Justice Statistics, nearly 78 percent of those incarcerated as of 2003 had not received a high school diploma compared to only 67 percent of the general population (Harlow). Not having a high school diploma coupled with a record of incarceration make it extremely difficult for people in this situation to secure employment upon release from prison. Often, this barrier to finding work leads to more crime and recidivism rates for those affected. Society foots a bill of $260,000 per person who does not graduate from high school "in lost earnings, taxes, and productivity" over the course of their lives, according to the Annie E. Casey foundation, and this does not account for people who are incarcerated (Feister 2010). In fiscal year 2015, the average annual cost for an inmate was nearly $32,000, which reaches the $260,000 milestone after approximately eight years. In either case, this money is being spent on people who are then benefiting from society without contributing to it and has a strong correlation to whether or not a person has received a high school diploma (Kenney 46957).

One study showed that children who were not reading at grade level by third grade were four times more likely to not graduate from high school (Hernandez 2011). Access to a high-quality preschool program increases the chances that a child will be appropriately equipped to be reading on grade level by third grade (Center for Public Education). Of course, income and social strata contribute to whether a child will have access to such a program, which is why programs like ours are so important: they contribute to kindergarten readiness without parents having to spend a penny. If you consider the significant social impact a lack of a high school diploma can have, it emphasizes the importance of achieving this goal. Therefore, programs like Little University can have a significant and positive effect on society at large decades into the future, regardless of a family's income or background.

It may seem like a weighty responsibility, but on the other hand, if we are not the ones to shoulder it, who will?

WHERE WE ARE NOW

The pioneering efforts of the librarians who established Every Child Ready to Read @ Your Library in the early 2000s paved the way for programming like ours to exist. The research and implementation of this program made library storytimes more educationally robust by providing librarians with the tools necessary to explain to parents why we do what we do in those storytimes. Read, write, sing, talk, and play, the central pillars of this program, are integral to early learning efforts. This important foundation led to our expansion on the concept of play in our Little University programming.

We are proud to report that Little University programming has found its stride not only within our library system, but within our city, as well. After years of establishing the program within our individual library branches, Little University is now able to be offered at other locations within the system. Expanding the program means that each library community in the city will receive the benefits of the Little University programming, which is, in turn, an enormous benefit to the children in those communities. It also means that there is more equal access to these programs when all libraries are able and encouraged to participate in them.

What you may find as you begin this journey is that there are few programs for this age group anywhere nearby. In our community, while the importance of school preparedness before third grade is well established and there is money to support that success, the city of Denver lacked the infrastructure to reach as many children in that age group as was desired. When Little University grew to the point of being recognized by the city as a legitimate program with the numbers and results to support that claim, the city preferred to transfer the money earmarked for this age group to us. This additional funding is making Little University expansion possible, and having the support of the city means that the program will continue to thrive for years to come.

While it is incredibly exciting to have support from the city, it is worth reiterating that library staff members at all levels have to be on board with this programming in order for it to be successful. Having city agencies support program expansion is one thing, but it is of critical importance that library staff be willing to do the work involved to get these programs off the ground. As you are considering this programming in your libraries, please bear this in mind as none of these programs can be successful in a vacuum. If that means a shift in staff priorities or a reevaluation of current library practices, then be aware of that possibility. If now is not the right time for your library, try not to lose heart. There are many ways early learning programming can happen, even if it is not formally a Little University program.

You can start small when creating programming for this age group. If formal programs will not work, try transforming some of the DIY options into take-home ideas for families. Simple handouts after a storytime can provide just enough inspiration for families to continue learning on their own at home. Keeping these handouts available all the time in your children's area can ensure that anyone in your library will benefit: not just those attending storytime.

Your library may grant you access to e-mail and/or social media as a means of communicating with your customers outside of the library. You can use this platform to encourage learning and growth by posting messages, videos, and ideas on a regular basis. These posts can get families thinking about learning even on days they are not in the library, thus inspiring more of the feelings and behaviors intended by Little University programs.

The intent of this book is to provide you with an outline for and inspiration to create or expand upon similar early literacy programming in your own library. Whether you have been thinking about this programming for years or are just beginning to consider it now does not matter: as long as you have the intent to provide quality programming to young children and their families and have support in doing so, you will be successful. If we have learned anything from our experiences, it is that the amount of heart you give to the project is the most critical component. Each program will improve organically, and each year will build upon the last.

Depending on your own communities, you may discover that there is money to be found to support programming of this type. That does not necessarily mean that it comes from city coffers, however. Individuals in the community who have income to support initiatives like this may be incredibly excited to do so. There may be grants or other community funding that can be obtained to get programs like this off the ground. If you think outside of the box and have data and interest to support your claims, you may be surprised by which people or organizations share your vision for engaging our youngest library users.

As you are considering approaching organizations in your community to request funding, whether they are for profit or not, make sure that you do your research. What does the organization stand for? To whom have they donated money in the past? Do they have any requirements for requesting money? If they give you money, is it a onetime thing or can it be renewed each year? What requirements are there for ensuring that any money is being used appropriately? When you have done your due diligence, you are ensuring that you are not wasting anyone's time (including your own) and that you enter into any meeting with as much knowledge as possible. Organizations will notice and appreciate this, and it may improve your chances of receiving the funding or other support you seek. For examples of elevator speeches to use to pitch this program within and around your library community, please see Appendix A at the end of the book.

MAINTAINING RELEVANCE

Receiving outside funding for your program series will set you up well to maintain relevance in your community, as most funders require some type of assessment and evaluation of how their funding was spent. Impacts of their funding can be measured, and future plans can be made based on the information provided in program evaluations.

For Kristin, for example, receiving private funding for her Little University program series necessitated an annual assessment and review of the programming she was offering. Was it repetitive, or was it different from the year before? What benefits did repeated programs offer participants, and how did new experiences benefit participants? What programs brought in the largest numbers of participants, and what programs did participants ask for again and again?

Whether or not your program series is funded by a source that requires ongoing assessment and evaluation, building this practice into your program series is critical to its success and future expansion.

Assessment and evaluation can occur in many ways, and we recommend several concurrent methods to keep you on track as you develop and build your early learning program series. To start, simply observing your program participants during their experience and chatting with the caregivers afterward will give you valuable information. Are all participants equally engaged, or are only the English speakers able to effectively participate? Are the children comfortable and curious? Anxious? Bored? When chatting after the program, was it fun and funny?

Noting the reactions of the participants will give you clear markers of where your program series is at present and will give you data that you can utilize to determine its future direction. Engaged and interested families indicate that your program is right on target. Bewildered or hesitant families might suggest that you have started a little bit further out than where they are comfortable, and you might need to dilute your offerings a bit before building back up. Skeptical or bored families might show you they are already familiar with your current program selection and are ready for something more complex and involved.

It is also valuable to simply ask your families: Did they enjoy this? Had they done this before? Had they had a similar experience elsewhere from which this one differed slightly in a better way? For example, many families adore visiting the local zoo and so might find a live animals program similar, but better, since children can see the animals outside the cages and perhaps even touch one!

These simple methods of assessment and evaluation will provide valuable information for both you and your financial supporters as you develop and build your early learning program series. From there, the challenge becomes ensuring that your program series continues to be relevant to your community. This is where more formal evaluation may be helpful.

Formally evaluating a program series such as Little University can be a tricky thing. The key is to identify the purpose of the evaluation. Are we evaluating to demonstrate that children have learned something through this program series? That caregivers have learned something? That families are relying on this program to prepare for school success? These are all difficult to measure. For our purposes, what we have settled on is this: we evaluate our program series to determine whether our early learners have had *the opportunity* to learn something new through our programs, and likewise whether our caregivers have had *the opportunity* to learn something new (either alongside their child, or about their child). From there, we can extrapolate that our program series is *a part of* preparing young children for success in school.

We do this in two ways. The first is by building a program series with a wide variety of learning opportunities—as many as possible!—which you read about in Chapters 3 and 4. From our program plans, we can demonstrate the vast number of different learning opportunities available to our communities.

Second, we offer a survey to our caregivers at two points during the year. The survey simply asks if their child has tried something new during one of our programs and what they have tried. The survey also gives caregivers an opportunity to share whether they have tried something new and, if so, what that was. Caregivers are also invited to share whether they have observed anything specific about their child during a Little University program, such as a new skill or a particular enjoyment of a specific program topic.

A quick note on surveying: we suggest introducing surveys to your program participants only after your program series is well established. Building a rapport with your families that includes trust is critical before asking for information about their young children. We also strongly suggest incentivizing taking the survey with something that will encourage learning at home. At Kristin's location, families who take the survey can exchange the completed version for a board book or a set of flashcards to take home and enjoy with their children. This is because, quite simply, juggling small children, diaper bags, snacks, water bottles, baby bottles, stuffies, and whatever else is needed to carry to a library program is enough of a task without trying to manage a sheet of paper and a pen along with it! Children are hopefully occupied selecting the incentive just long enough for parents to complete the questionnaire.

It is also worth noting that translating the surveys may be necessary as well to ensure that all caregivers can participate in this information-gathering process.

Surveying is no simple task, either for you or for your families! Still, the results are quite valuable for both you and for your funders. Taken together with informal assessments like chatting with caregivers, observing program participation, and hard data such as program attendance, surveys will round out your assessment and evaluation and ensure that your program series continues to maintain relevance for your community.

WHAT TO DO NEXT?

So you have read through the book, considered your library's budget, become inspired by some of the ideas in Chapters 3 and 4 and are starting to determine how a program like this might be able to exist within your library. That is very exciting! We sincerely hope that something like this will work in your library and your community regardless of any restraints that you may have.

However, in all reality, it is possible that a program like ours may not be able to be established in your community in the manner we have suggested. Please do not lose heart! If that is the case, there are many other ways in which you can implement our ideas in order to provide meaningful programming for your library users.

If you are not able to add another program to your library's repertoire due to staffing or other restrictions, consider augmenting one or more of your existing storytime programs. This can mean including a craft or activity after storytime is over, including movement or other activities within the storytime itself, or even just providing take-home activities and instructions for families. If you are looking for inspiration, librarians the world over have shared their expertise on the Internet, often for free. Take advantage of this! Our community is one that shares readily and often, improving our services by leaps and bounds for our library users.

Another alternative is doing special events at strategic times during the year. Do you participate in summer reading programs? Perhaps you could make a Little University program part of your summer programming. Do you have opportunities to do special programming throughout the year? Maybe it would work best for your library to have a Little University program once a month or once a quarter to coincide with other community events or to take place when staffing is available.

However it works for your library is unequivocally the best option. Whether it is on a weekday or a weekend, in the morning or in the afternoon, with a large budget or a small one, the most important thing is that you are working to improve your community and are doing so in a way that is *sustainable*. The longevity of the program is what will ensure that results are seen. If that means starting small and building from there, then do that. You can always improve the program when you start from something manageable.

Children learn both from exposure to new experiences *and* from repetition of experiences. This second statement is critical to remember moving forward.

LOOKING AHEAD: HOW TO CONTINUE BUILDING YOUR PROGRAM

Early Learning Progress Report

- This could be offered once a year, once a "semester," once a season, or once a month. We like the idea of once a "semester," as it both plays into our Little University moniker and helps orient caregivers to a school schedule.

- The progress report could be designed in a number of ways: spin off from a school report card format, a Bingo-style card, or a simple list.

- From here, you would list your program categories, much the same way as we did in Chapters 3 and 4: a movement program, a music program, and so on. We encourage you to list both the name of the program category and a picture along with the name.

- Caregivers would simply check off each time they attended a program category. Ideally, by the end of the semester, families would have experienced at least one program in each category.

- Hopefully, there will be funding to offer an incentive for completing the progress report, like a soccer ball, a watercolor set, or a kids' yoga mat. All will encourage continued learning at home.

Surveys and Incentives

- We mentioned surveys in more detail earlier, but it is worth mentioning again as all our locations will soon be surveying caregivers about their families' experiences in Little University.

- Ensure that your survey questions ask for the information you want. Asking about children's developmental skills might seem logical, but in reality it cannot be credited to your program series. We cannot determine for certain that a child learned left and right from a Little University soccer program or from a parent consistently articulating this while putting on the child's shoes. What we *can* determine, however, is that a child had an opportunity to learn left and right, or to play soccer, or to develop gross motor skills, by asking if the child has attended this type of program, and if so, whether it was a new experience.

- As with the progress report, offering an incentive here is an excellent addition. An incentive will serve at once to validate the caregivers' time in taking the survey and encourage ongoing early learning at home.

Little University for Grown-Ups

- This idea is a special add-on session for caregivers and is designed to build upon what their children have learned during Little University.

Think of it as kind of a behind-the-scenes look into what skills children are learning while participating in these early learning programs as well as an offering for caregivers to learn new things.

- "Little U for Grown-Ups" could be offered monthly or simply at the start or end of a program "semester" or season.

- Programs might include a look into fine and gross motor skills, a discussion of what children need for kindergarten success, a fair of preschools in the community, fire safety and stranger danger, saving money for college, and self-care for caregivers. Other options might steer toward fun topics such as daddy-daughter hair workshops, sneaking healthy foods into your child's diet, apps and screen time for this age group, and educational games and toys currently on the market.

- Two considerations are worth noting here: translation and childcare. As we currently offer Little U for Grown-Ups in Kristin's location, translation thus far has not been a major issue. Families who do not speak English primarily in their home tend to send the one caregiver comfortable with the language or simply attend the program and get what they can out of it! With childcare, almost all of the Little U for Grown-Ups programs allow for children to attend along with caregivers. Sometimes we offer extension activities for the children during Little U for Grown-Ups, or caregivers bring along toys and snacks to entertain children while the caregivers learn.

- These sessions have, to date, been met with high attendance and measurable success. Caregivers love the learning extension; demonstrating to their young children that they, too, love to learn goes far to instill a love of learning from a very young age!

Kindergarten Readiness Checklist

- Sometimes, Kristin and Mary approach their Little University program planning from the perspective of being a parent as well as that of being a professional. As a parent whose child was preparing to enter Kindergarten, Kristin was certainly aware of the vague concept that her son should have a certain level of preparedness for this transition, but what that preparedness entailed was surprisingly difficult to find.

- Your early learning program series might grow to include some information about what children need to be successful in kindergarten in order to help caregivers navigate this nebulous time.

- This could be as simple as including an item each week that children need to know before kindergarten when you introduce your program. For example, you might highlight to caregivers that it is certainly fine if they need to step out for a break during the program, and that in fact children will need to know how to ask for a bathroom break when they enter kindergarten.

- This could also be as involved as providing an actual checklist of hard and soft skills children need to know before entering kindergarten either from your local schools or from information you find through research. You would hopefully be able to tie many of these skills to learning opportunities provided by your program series!

- This could be as complex as inviting guest speakers to your library, either as a Little U for Grown-Ups session or as a special program, to discuss kindergarten readiness with your caregivers. Speakers will hopefully address developmental milestones such as counting and building block towers, as well as social-emotional learning such as empathy and raising a hand to ask a question.

- Beginning school is a huge transition for both caregivers and children, and using your Little University program series to help ease uncertainty around that transition is an outstanding way to support the families in your community as they move on.

Graduation

- Along the same lines, honoring time children have spent attending your early learning program series is an excellent way to usher their transition out of the preschool age group and into the school age group.

- A graduation ceremony or recognition is both adorable and beneficial for the families with whom you have worked during their child's early learning development. If nothing else, honoring their repeated program attendance with a marker of completion validates and highlights the importance of their child's learning during your program series.

- Graduation might include the aforementioned progress reports, or simply highlight one or two of the child's favorite early learning programs. Caregivers might want to weigh in on growth they have observed from attending your program series, or simply allow you to recognize their child's transition from preschool to kindergarten. Perhaps your library will allow you to put up a display to recognize the Little University graduates or simply allow staff time to attend a small ceremony you put together.

- Maybe you gift your Little University graduates items off the local schools' kindergarten school supply lists or simply provide them with a calendar of library events for school-aged children that they are now eligible to attend.

- Whatever form it may take, recognizing the transition out of your early learning program series is also an excellent way to recognize all the work the child engaged in *during* your early learning program series.

IN SUMMARY

We provided a wealth of information in this book, and so in conclusion, we will boil that information down to a few key bullet points to remember when beginning your own early learning program series:

- Assess your community.
- Plan in advance.
- Market effectively.
- Engage community partners.
- Build a list of program options.
- Master DIY programming options.

It is possible that you already have early learning programming at your library location and have read our book to expand the horizons of your existing program series. If that is the case, wonderful! Please make use of our newest early learning program initiatives and ideas.

Learning through play is a fun, engaging, and uniting effort in bringing young children and their families together in the library while supporting skills required to be successful readers. Coupled with storytime, programs with this focus strengthen learning channels and encourage a love of reading and learning. This self-driven desire to engage with the wider world is critical to success in school and in life, and it can begin to be cultivated from birth. We are thrilled that you have joined us on our journey by investing in this book, and we are enthusiastic to see where you take these ideas within your own community.

Above all, we hope that this text has engaged your feelings about libraries and early learning. Perhaps your perspective has shifted or expanded from what it was before picking up this book. Ours has certainly been altered from what it was before beginning our early learning program series.

As a result, on a regular basis now, we hear families with babies, toddlers, and preschoolers meet live animals and exclaim about them in English, Arabic, Korean, Hindi, Spanish, and other languages. We watch children with learning disabilities' faces light up when ukuleles are distributed that they are allowed to hold and play. We help parents with designer handbags get elbow deep in finger paints with their babies, and grandparents from out of town patiently mix homemade Play-Doh with their toddler grandchildren. We watch mothers in burkas play soccer with their preschool-aged children alongside suburban dads cheering a bit too loudly from the "sidelines." We sit quietly while families enjoy a savasana and a cuddle with their little ones.

In short, during every early learning program, we are reminded of how we have embraced the potential a library has to foster early learning, a profound sense of community, and an ongoing love of learning for all the families our libraries serve. We hope that this book has enabled the same sort of perspective shift we experienced, for you.

APPENDIX A

Elevator Speeches

To encourage upper management to adopt the idea:

- Little University would be an excellent addition to our preexisting library programming because it will help bring our community together with the common goal of educating our youngest library users. Regardless of language or cultural background, we as library staff can facilitate connection through play when a shared language may not exist.

- Even though we do not have money budgeted for this project, there are ways we can use the resources we already have to get Little University off the ground. Once we establish that the program can be successful with a limited budget, we can make a case to have more money given to us to keep it moving forward.

- A program like Little University is critical to the success of the children in our service area. What they learn here will help them be prepared to enter kindergarten and do well in school going forward. This is of immeasurable importance to the health and longevity of our society, as well.

To get other library staff interested in promoting and participating in the program:

- Little University is a complement to our traditional storytime programming, so we encourage families to attend both programs, if they can. While storytime focuses on books and singing, Little University is all about learning through experiences and play. Here is our upcoming schedule of events to hand out to families at the desk!

- Little University is open to all families with children under age five. Not only is it a great learning opportunity for families, but it also gives neighbors a chance to meet and get to know one another. Even if it's a program that a family has done before, repetition is the key to retaining new knowledge. Plus, children enjoy programs even more as they improve their skills!

To encourage attendance from library users:

- Little University is an excellent addition to the storytime you're already attending! Your children will learn new things by playing and experiencing them firsthand. We even have a special visit from the zoo with animals your child can touch!

- It's OK if you don't have time to attend storytime during the week. We have a special program called Little University that is specifically designed to be available when you are. Here is our schedule. We would love to see you there!

- Little University is a free program where families can learn together through play and other hands-on experiences. Children will learn skills that complement what they are learning in storytime, so attending both programs is ideal!

To secure funding, donations, and participation from community organizations:

- Did you know that whether a child is reading on grade level by the time he or she reaches third grade is a direct predictor of high school graduation? Little University helps get children and their families on the right path to literacy from birth in a hands-on, experiential way. Support for this program helps ensure that we are able to reach families of all income levels and backgrounds to give their children the strongest start we can.

- There are very few free programs where families of all means can come together and educate their children. As libraries have limited budgets and many needs, support from you allows Little University to continue providing meaningful experiences for the libraries that rely upon it.

- Community support is integral to the success of Little University, both financially and through programming. When the community is committed to a child's education, that child and his or her family feel support from many sides, thereby encouraging that child to continue to learn and enjoy doing so.

APPENDIX B

Need to DIY? Twenty Titles to Build an Early Learning Program Series Reference Collection

ART

Kohl, MaryAnn F. (2012). *First Art for Toddlers and Twos: Open Ended Art Experiences.* Lewisville, NC: Gryphon House.
Saltzburg, Barney. (2010). *Beautiful Oops!* New York: Workman Publishing.

HEALTH AND NUTRITION

Karmel, Annabel. (2008). *The Toddler Cookbook.* London, England: DK Children.
Woolmer, Annabelle. (2017). *The Tickle Fingers Toddler Cookbook: Hands-on Fun in the Kitchen for 1 to 4s.* London, England: Random House UK.

MINDFULNESS

Engel, Christine. (2018). *ABC for Me: ABC for Mindful Me: ABCs for a Happy, Healthy Body and Mind.* London, England: Walter Foster, Jr.
Snel, Eline. (2013). *Sitting Still Like a Frog: Mindfulness Exercises for Kids (and Their Parents).* Boulder, CO: Shambala Center.
Verde, Susan. (2017). *I Am Peace: A Book of Mindfulness.* New York: Harry N. Abrams.

Willey, Kira. (2017). *Breathe Like a Bear: 30 Mindful Moments for Kids to Feel Calm and Focused Anytime, Anywhere*. New York: Rodale Kids.

MUSIC AND MOVEMENT

Gill, Jim. (2013). *Jim Gill Sings the Sneezing Song and Other Contagious Tunes: 20th Anniversary Edition* (Audio CD). Jim Gill Music.

STEM

Barbre, Jean. (2017). *Baby Steps to STEM*. Corona, CA: Redleaf Press.
Beaty, Andrea. (2016). *Ada Twist, Scientist*. New York: Harry N. Abrams.
Brunelle, Lynn. (2016). *Big Science for Little People: 52 Activities to Help You & Your Child Discover the Wonders of Science (An Official Geek Mama Guide)*. Boulder, CO: Roost Books.
Hesselbirth, Joyce. (2018). *Mapping Sam*. New York: Greenwillow Books.
McKellar, Danica. (2017). *Goodnight Numbers*. New York: Crown Books for Young Readers.
Spires, Ashley. (2014). *The Most Magnificent Thing*. Toronto, Canada: Kids Can Press.

YOGA

Engel, Christine. (2016). *ABC for Me: ABC Yoga: Join Us and the Animals Out in Nature and Learn Some Yoga!* London, England: Walter Foster, Jr.
Gates, Miriam. (2016). *Good Morning Yoga: A Pose by Pose Wake Up Story*. Louisville, CO: Sounds True Publishing.
Gates, Miriam. (2015). *Good Night Yoga: A Pose by Pose Bedtime Story*. Louisville, CO: Sounds True Publishing.
Hinder, Sarah Jane. (2017). *Yoga Bug: Simple Poses for Little Ones*. Louisville, CO: Sounds True Publishing.
Verde, Susan. (2015). *I Am Yoga*. New York: Harry N. Abrams.

APPENDIX C

Program Flyer Template

Your Program Series Title
Early Learning Programs for ages Birth-Preschool & Caregivers

Day & Time | Location

DATE: PROGRAM TITLE with PRESENTER'S NAME
Early learning skill tied into program topic + brief description of the program.

DATE: PROGRAM TITLE with PRESENTER'S NAME
Early learning skill tied into program topic + brief description of the program.

DATE: PROGRAM TITLE with PRESENTER'S NAME
Early learning skill tied into program topic + brief description of the program.

SPECIAL EVENT OR PROGRAM ADD-ON
Provide a brief description here.

DATE: PROGRAM TITLE with PRESENTER'S NAME
Early learning skill tied into program topic + brief description of the program. Anything special your families need to know? Be sure to include it here!

DATE: PROGRAM TITLE with PRESENTER'S NAME
Early learning skill tied into program topic + brief description of the program.

Get creative!

Make a logo to brand your program!

Length of the program
Questions? Call us! 555.867.5309

Be sure to credit your financial sponsors & donors!

LITTLE UNIVERSITY

Early Learning Programs for ages Birth-Preschool & Caregivers

SATURDAYS @ 10:30AM | SCHLESSMAN FAMILY BRANCH LIBRARY

SEPT 1: CREATURE MEET & GREET with NATURE'S EDUCATORS
Live animals!! Learning about these animals will introduce your
little ones to new vocabulary words. We will meet three live
animals and may be able to touch one at the end of the program.

SEPT 8: INSTRUMENT EXPLORERS with ENTHUSIASTIC MUSIC
Making music together is a great way to bond with your little
ones! We will have fun singing and dancing during this program.

SEPT 15: DEVELOPMENTAL PLAY with KIDSENSE
Work with an occupational therapist to learn play-based
activities to encourage little ones to meet developmental
milestones!

> **LITTLE U 102: DEVELOPMENTAL PLAY**
> Have questions about meeting specific milestones or
> addressing specific challenges? Our occupational
> therapist will present a few ideas and then
> take questions!

SEPT 22: "COOKING" with THE EDIBLE REVOLUTION
We are going to "cook!" Little ones will develop
fine motor skills while making a healthy recipe.
Please notify instructor(s) of any allergies!!

SEPT 29: STORYTIME YOGA with MISS SHANTI
Yoga helps little ones build a mind-body
connection and practice self-control. We'll bring
a story to life with simple yoga poses. No
experience necessary; this is just for fun!

PROGRAMS ARE 25 MINUTES.
QUESTIONS? CALL US! 720.865.0000

Bibliography

Bouffard, Suzanne. (2017). *The Most Important Year: Pre-Kindergarten and the Future of Our Children.* New York: Avery (a division of Penguin Random House).

"Building on Success." *Every Child Ready to Read. Read. Learn. Grow.* American Library Association. http://www.everychildreadytoread.org/.

Celano, Donna C., and Susan B. Neuman. (2015, April). "Libraries Emerging as Leaders in Parent Engagement." *Phi Delta Kappan*, vol. 96 (7), pp. 30–35. doi:10.1177/0031721715579037.

Center for Public Education. (2015, March). *Learning to Read, Reading to Learn: Why Third-Grade Is a Pivotal Year for Mastering Literacy.* http://www.centerforpubliceducation.org/system/files/Leading%20 to%20Read%20%28Full%20report%29_0.pdf.

Christaskis, Erika. (2017). *The Importance of Being Little: What Young Children Really Need from Grown-Ups.* New York: Penguin Books.

Deruy, Emily. (2016). "Learning through Play." *The Atlantic,* September 13. https://www.theatlantic.com/education/archive/2016/09/ learning-through-play/499703/.

ECRR Chart. https://static1.squarespace.com/static/531bd3f2e4b0a09d95 833bfc/t/568c4ba3bfe87399730708f2/1452034979939/elcompprac chart.pdf.

Feister, L. (2010). *Early Warning! Why Reading by the End of Third Grade Matters.* Baltimore, MD: Annie E. Casey Foundation.

Ginsburg, Kenneth R. (2007, January). "The Importance of Play in Promoting Healthy Child Development and Maintaining Strong Parent Child Bonds." *Pediatrics,* vol. 119 (1), pp. 182–191. doi:10.1542/ peds.2006–2697.

Harlow, Caroline Wolf. (2003). "Education and Correctional Populations." *Bureau of Justice Statistics*, April 15. www.bjs.gov/index.cfm?ty=pbdetail&iid=814.

Hernandez, D. J. (2011). *Double Jeopardy: How Third-Grade Reading Skills and Poverty Influence High School Graduation*. Baltimore, MD: Annie E. Casey Foundation.

"Home Page." *Every Child Ready to Read. Read. Learn. Grow.* American Library Association. everychildreadytoread.org/.

Kamenetz, Anya. (2018). "5 Proven Benefits of Play." *National Public Radio,* August 31. https://www.npr.org/sections/ed/2018/08/31/642567651/5-proven-benefits-of-play.

Kenney, Kathleen M. (2016). "Department of Justice." *Federal Register*, vol. 81 (138), July 19, p. 46957.

Klass, Perri. (2018). "Let Kids Play." *New York Times,* August 20. https://www.nytimes.com/2018/08/20/well/family/let-kids-play.html.

Lahey, Jessica. (2014). "Why Free Play Is the Best Summer School." *The Atlantic,* June 20. https://www.theatlantic.com/education/archive/2014/06/for-better-school-results-clear-the-schedule-and-let-kids-play/373144/.

Lobley, Pam. (2016). *Why Can't We Just Play: What I Did When I Realized My Kids Were Too Busy to Play*. Sanger, CA: Familius.

Louv, Richard. (2008). *Last Child in the Woods: Saving Children from Nature-Deficit Disorder*. Chapel Hill, NC: Algonquin Books.

Neuman, Susan B., Naomi Moland, and Donna Celano. (2017). *Bringing Literacy Home: An Evaluation of the Every Child Ready to Read Program*. Chicago: American Library Association, pp. 1–77.

Sampson, Scott D. (2015). *How to Raise a Wild Child: The Art and Science of Falling in Love with Nature*. Boston, MA: Houghton, Mifflin, Harcourt.

Tough, Paul. (2013). *How Children Succeed: Grit, Curiosity, and the Hidden Power of Character*. Boston, MA: Houghton, Mifflin, Harcourt.

Yogman, Michael, Andrew Garner, Jeffrey Hutchinson, Kathy Hirsh-Pasek, and Roberta Michnick Golinkoff. (2018, August). *The Power of Play: A Pediatric Role in Enhancing Development in Young Children*. Itasca, IL: American Academy of Pediatrics.

Index

About the Authors

Kristin Grabarek has worked for more than 10 years developing relevant library services and programs for learners from birth through early adolescence at the Denver Public Library and at the Auraria Library on the University of Colorado-Denver campus. She published "Anonymity versus Perceived Patron Identity in Virtual Reference Transcripts," with Karen Sobel (*Public Services Quarterly,* Volume 8, Issue 4, 2012) and "Teen Asset Mapping" (2015), a project with PLA Fellow and Denver Public Library city librarian Michelle Jeske, before turning her professional attention to our youngest learners. Kristin implemented Little University, an early learning program beyond traditional storytime, four years ago at her branch of the Denver Public Library system and is now assisting in its expansion to multiple branches throughout the system. Her professional interest is in maintaining public libraries' relevancy to families by offering play-based, innovative programming that directly promotes individualized learning.

Mary R. Lanni is a library professional in Denver, Colorado, providing library and programming services for all ages for over five years. She has worked with children in a variety of capacities over the last 17 years, from teaching Irish stepdancing, to being a children's museum educator, to leading storytime. These experiences have formed her understanding of the myriad ways through which children learn, and she implements this knowledge in her library programming for children and their families. She has served on the Steering Committee for the Colorado Libraries for Early Literacy for the past three years, serving as the chair of the Communications Committee and adding six more languages to the Storyblocks training videos, a project executed in collaboration with the Colorado State Library and Rocky Mountain PBS. She is passionate about spreading the message of the importance of early learning to the families of young children and the communities in which they live.